MY RENDANG ISN'T CRISPY
and Other Favourite Malaysian Dishes

ZALEHA KADIR OLPIN

Marshall Cavendish
Cuisine

Cover shots and food photography by Mireya González
Street photography by David Olpin

Copyright © 2019 Marshall Cavendish International (Asia) Private Limited

First published 2019
This paperback edition 2022
ISBN 978 981 5009 85 9

Published By Marshall Cavendish Cuisine
An imprint of Marshall Cavendish International

A member of the
Times Publishing Group

Other Marshall Cavendish Offices:
Marshall Cavendish Corporation, 800 Westchester Ave, Suite N-641,
Rye Brook, NY 10573, USA • Marshall Cavendish International (Thailand)
Co Ltd, 253 Asoke, 16th Flr, Sukhumvit 21 Road, Klongtoey Nua, Wattana,
Bangkok 10110, Thailand • Marshall Cavendish (Malaysia) Sdn Bhd,
Times Subang, Lot 46, Subang Hi-Tech Industrial Park, Batu Tiga,
40000 Shah Alam, Selangor Darul Ehsan, Malaysia

Printed in Singapore

Braving a tropical storm,
a typical scene in my kampung.

Contents

Fish and Seafood

Ikan Masak Asam
Fish in Tamarind Sauce 46

Ikan Singgang
East Coast Fish Broth 48

Kari Ikan Mak
Mum's Fish Curry 50

Sambal Udang
Prawn Sambal 52

Sambal Ikan Hijau
Fish in Green Sambal 54

Sotong Sos Tiram
Squid in Oyster Sauce 56

Ketupat Sotong
Malaysian-style Stuffed Squid 58

Ikan Masak Masam Manis
Sweet and Sour Fish 60

Lemak Cili Padi Udang
Prawn and Pineapple Curry 62

Meat and Poultry

Rendang Ayam MasterChef UK
My "Non Crispy" MasterChef UK
Chicken Rendang 66

Ayam Golek
Malaysian-style Roast Chicken 68

Gulai Pahang
Pahang-style Curry 70

Ayam Masak Hitam
Zen Chicken 72

Ayam Masak Merah
Chicken Sambal 74

Ayam Goreng, The Olpins
Olpin's Fried Chicken 76

Kari Ayam
Chicken Curry 78

Rendang Daging Mudah
Basic Beef Rendang 80

Rendang Opor Pahang
Rendang from My Home Town 82

Rendang Tok Kak Uteh
Grandma's Rendang 84

Sup Kambing Mamak
Spicy Mamak-style Lamb Soup 86

Vegetables, Salads and Pickles

Acar Timun dan Lobak
Cucumber and Carrot Pickle 90

Acar Nenas Saffron
Saffron and Pineapple Pickle 92

Jelatah Mangga dengan Lada Benggala MasterChef UK
My MasterChef UK Mango and Pepper Salad 92

Kacang Panjang Goreng Berlada
Stir-fried Spicy Long Beans 94

Kobis Goreng dengan Telur
Stir-fried Cabbage with Egg 94

Kacang Buncis Goreng dengan Sos Tiram
Stir-fried French Beans with Oyster Sauce 96

Solok Lada
Stuffed Green Chillies 96

Light Bites and Snacks

Satay Ayam
Chicken Satay 100

Katlet Ikan MasterChef UK
My MasterChef UK Fish Cutlets 102

Kerabu Daging
Beef Salad 104

Tauhu Sumbat
Stuffed Tofu 106

Popiah Sayur
Vegetable Spring Rolls 108

Karipap Pusing
Spiral Curry Puffs 110

Tembosa
Fish and Coconut Curry Puffs 112

Keropok Lekor
Malaysian Fish Sausage 114

Otak-Otak
Grilled Fish Cakes in Banana Leaf 116

Cucur Udang
Prawn Fritters 118

Pulut Sambal
Sticky Rice Bon Bon 120

Lempeng Kelapa
Coconut Pancakes 122

Sweet Treats

Kek Pisang Kampung
Kampung-style Banana Cake 126

Kuih Bom
Deep-fried Glutinous Rice Flour Balls with Sweet Coconut Filling 128

Kuih Ketayap
Pandan Crepes with Sweet Coconut Filling 130

Onde-Onde
Glutinous Rice Flour Balls with Palm Sugar Filling 132

Sagu Gula Melaka
Sago with Palm Sugar and Coconut Cream 134

Sauces and Condiments

Keropok Chilli Sauce
Sos Keropok 138

Sweet Chilli Sauce
Sos Cili Manis 138

Sweet Soy Sauce Dip
Sambal Kicap 139

Tomato Sambal
Sambal Tomato 139

Peanut Sauce
Kuah Kacang 140

Nasi Lemak Sambal Bawang
Sambal Nasi Lemak 141

Above: Cooking rendang with Vicki Treadell, British High Commissioner to Australia (formerly to Malaysia), outside my home in Kuantan.

Foreword

Zaleha and I first connected in April 2018 in the Twittersphere over #RendangGate. I was the British High Commissioner to Malaysia at the time. I, like many Malaysians who know and take pride in great Malaysian cuisine, felt I had to come to Zaleha's defence over accusations that her chicken rendang was not crispy enough. There had also been some ill-judged comments about the origins of the dish not being Malaysian. I therefore tweeted that "Rendang is an iconic Malaysian national dish not to be confused with Indonesian options. It can be chicken, lamb or beef. It is never crispy and should not be confused with the fried chicken sometimes served with *nasi lemak*". I personally love *nasi lemak* for breakfast!

We then met in May 2018 in London and talked food. In this conversation, we shared experiences of finding ourselves in foreign countries and missing our favourite foods. When my family migrated from Malaysia to the UK in 1968, this was the case. My mother had to learn to recreate our favourite family dishes and she struggled to find the ingredients in British supermarkets. She, like Zaleha, had to write to her sisters and friends to get recipes and tips. This resonated with Zaleha's own experiences and we found much in common. Indeed, so enthused were we at sharing such experiences, we came up with the crazy idea that we should cook together when Zaleha next visited family in Malaysia. We fulfilled that promise three months later in August 2018, in the delightful semi-rural setting of Kampung Baru, Kuantan. Zaleha taught me to cook her chicken rendang in the open air under rambutan trees outside her family's kampung house.

And now the great privilege of providing this foreword.

The recipes Zaleha shares in this book are special. They are the dishes of home, infused not just with the aromatic spices they include, but with memories of family and friends. We cook not just for sustenance but for love, for the people we care for.

My mother told me that food is the first happiness, a pleasure we discover before others. A pleasure that is both a life force and lifelong. A meal can be a simple necessity, to eat to live. But it can be much more: it can be intimate and private, a huge public celebration, a family affair, a feast, a fun night with friends, a way to soothe, a means to build and nurture relationships, a way to offer kindness and hospitality. In my profession as a diplomat, food, or what I call gastrodiplomacy, is a vital tool. What we serve, how we serve it and with whom we share and enjoy the meal, can make for the most convivial and memorable occasions. It eases conversations and helps us to build trust and understanding.

Having been born in Malaysia, I relish this new addition to our culinary understanding of classic dishes. Many of my personal favourites, like *mee goreng mamak* and *sambal udang*, are to be found here and, of course, the very dish — chicken rendang — that brought Zaleha and I together and united an entire nation. I look forward to recreating these dishes in my own kitchen and sharing the results with others. Thank you, Zaleha, for sharing your recipes with all of us.

Vicki Treadell
British High Commissioner to Australia
(formerly to Malaysia)

Top: The Kuantan River flows through the city of Kuantan and out to the South China Sea. *Right:* Kuantan has some of the loveliest beaches along Malaysia's East Coast. *Above:* With my family. *Inset:* With my late mum.

Acknowledgements

Writing this book has been one of the most challenging things I have ever had to do. Without the constant encouragement from the people I love, I would never have taken up and completed this task. For this, I am truly grateful.

My late mother instilled in me a passion for food. She taught me to cook and I wish she was around to hold this book, kiss me on the cheek and say, "Well done!" I miss you, mum.

To my husband David, thank you for believing in me. You have the patience of a saint and you are my rock!

Special love goes to my daughters, Aiman and Sofea, who encouraged me to sign up for MasterChef UK. You two munchkins started me on this whole new chapter of my life and I am enjoying every moment of it! Thank you!

To my mentor, Puan Zaharah Othman (Kak Teh) from the *New Straits Times*, Malaysia. We clicked the moment we met. Thank you, Kak, for supporting me on this culinary journey.

To Puan Norzaini Abdul Hamid (Aunty Aini) who runs Aunty Aini's Garden Café in Malaysia. We both share the same passion for keeping the authenticity of Malaysian cuisine.

To Fatimah and Nafeesa, my partners in Malaysian Kitchen UK. You two are like sisters to me. It has been wonderful working with you. I could not have asked for more.

To my family members in Malaysia and Singapore, especially my sister-in-law, Rokiah, who helped hone my cooking skills. We may be separated by distance, but you are always close in my heart.

To BBC UK, Shine TV, the MasterChef UK judges and the crew, thank you for the most incredible journey. I am truly thankful.

To MasterChef Malaysia judge, Chef Johari Edrus, thank you for the support and kindness you showed me and my family.

Huge thanks to Dato Chef Wan, my cooking idol. I am also immensely grateful to Dato Chef Fazley for being there for me and Chef Norman Musa who always keeps in touch to see how I am getting along.

To my friends whom I met over the past two decades whilst travelling the globe. Thank you for introducing me to your cultures and foods.

To the team at Marshall Cavendish International (Asia). I never thought that I would ever get to write a cookbook, let alone be published by such a reputable publisher. Thank you, Lydia, for believing in me. When you approached me with this offer, I had to pinch myself to make sure I wasn't dreaming. Thank you for holding my hand and walking with me throughout this journey.

I would also like to thank my lovely photographer, Mireya González. We met by chance and it turned into such a wonderful partnership. I enjoyed every moment we spent styling and photographing the food, then eating it! You are simply amazing.

Last, but not least, a very big thank you to Liz at Liz Vidal Ceramics, Dr Ida Bakar, Aiman Hasnan, Daniela and Edu Ebner, Ana and Tim Coutts, Mariana and Marcos Malzone, and Mireya González for the generous loan of the props and tableware for the duration of the photography sessions.

Introduction

I was born in Kuantan, in the state of Pahang, East Malaysia. I grew up among seven siblings and we were cared for by nannies and drivers since my parents ran a busy family business that included restaurants and catering services. Although I grew up watching my parents, uncles and aunties work their magic with food, I was never interested in cooking. Instead, I used to work at the tills. As part of my training, however, I was made to stand and watch my mum cook her special rendang for hours after the restaurant closed! And never in a million years did I think I would one day stand in the MasterChef UK kitchen to present that very same dish to the judges, to the whole of the UK, and indeed, the world!

Before moving away from Malaysia two decades ago, I was ignorant about our traditional cooking methods. I took for granted the essence of cooking because the food I enjoyed was easily available, and it was more convenient to go to restaurants than labour at the stove to feed my small family. On top of that, I was working full-time, so why bother cooking?

When I moved to Australia, however, things changed. I had trouble finding authentic Malaysian food and I needed my fix of my favourite *nasi lemak* and curry noodles. And so, I had no choice but to learn to prepare them myself. This was back in the day before the convenience of video calls and I had to make long distance phone calls to ask my mum how to cook this and that. Can you imagine my phone bills? But it was all worth it because I was able to satisfy my food cravings and make my family happy. It was also then that I started to appreciate the intricacies of Malaysian cooking and experiment with different cuisines.

Given the nature of my husband's job as a marine engineer, we moved around a lot and wherever we went, I was able to introduce Malaysian food to our new friends and learn about their food and culture at the same time. This has made me aware that some ingredients may not be as easily available in some places. As such, in this book, I list the original herbs and spices used in Malaysia, and also suggest substitutes where necessary.

Some recipes may seem tedious, with a long list of ingredients, but once you familiarise yourself with the ingredients, you will find that cooking Malaysian food is as simple as any other cuisine you may be familiar with. To help with this, I have included a section to highlight ingredients essential in Malaysian cooking. I have also specially written the recipes with simple step-by-step instructions, and grouped the ingredients in order of use, so the recipes are easy to follow.

In Malay, we use the term, *agak-agak,* which means estimation. There are no precise measurements in our family recipes as ingredients were added based on experience. When working on this book, however, I made sure to measure and write down the quantities for every ingredient, so that anyone using the recipes would produce dishes similar in taste and flavour to mine. But remember, taste is subjective! There is always room for experimentation once you are comfortable with the method. If this is your first time trying your hand at Malaysian cooking, choose a recipe that really piques your interest. Don't worry about the lengthy method or unfamiliar ingredient names. Start by reading through the recipe, several times, if needed, then preparing all the ingredients and having them ready by your stove before you start cooking. Keep working at it and you will become a Malaysian food masterchef in no time!

Here's to a wonderful culinary journey through Malaysia! *Jemput makan!* (Let's eat!)

Zaleha Kadir Olpin
Makcik Rendang, a.k.a. the Rendang Lady
MasterChef UK Season 14 Contestant

Discussing gastrodiplomacy with Vicki Treadell.

A *muruku* stall at a busy street market in Bangsar, Kuala Lumpur.

Getting to Know Malaysia and Her Cuisine

Without delving too much into geography and history, let me try to explain a little about what has contributed to making Malaysian cuisine what it is today.

Located within South East Asia, Malaysia is made up of two geographical regions: West Malaysia and East Malaysia, which are divided by the South China Sea, and bordered by Thailand, Singapore, Indonesia and Brunei.

Historically, due to its strategic location, Malaysia (or the Malay Peninsula as it was then known) was a popular trade route for ships crossing the Indian Ocean. Indian, Arab and Chinese merchants plying these routes established themselves in Malaysia and integrated their cultures within the society. By the early 16th century, European interest in the region brought along the Portuguese (1511), the British, via the East India Company (1600), and the Dutch, via the Dutch East India Company (1646). The various influences from these different cultures created a multi-ethnic and multicultural society that defines Malaysia today.

A Celebration of Cultures and Cuisines

From a gastronomic point of view, Malaysia can be said to be one of the richest and most exciting countries where you can find many types of cuisine.

In the northern states, such as Perlis and Kedah, the food reflects Thai influence. In the popular tourist destination of Penang, the food is predominantly influenced by Chinese and Indian cuisine. To the south in Melaka, Peranakan, or Nyonya, food dominates the scene. In my home state of Pahang, the food remains very kampung-style, or traditional, with many seafood dishes due to its proximity to the coast.

Growing up in a small village, I was lucky to have lived in a diverse neighbourhood. My family is Malay, and we had Chinese and Indian neighbours. One of my fondest memories of childhood was receiving food from these neighbours.

My siblings and I always looked forward to the Chinese New Year when our Chinese neighbours would bake and share their pineapple tarts and other cookies, and of course present us with red packets (that contained money!) for good luck. During the Mid Autumn Festival, they would also make mooncakes, Chinese pastries filled with bean paste, and give us some. To this day, I still remember the distinct smell of Aunty Boon's cooking, as the garlic sizzled in the hot oil in her wok. She often invited us to her house for meals and we also shared our mum's cooking with her.

Griddle pancakes, a popular snack in Malaysia. Malaysians are spoilt for choice when it comes to seafood. Basting satay with a lemongrass brush.

During Diwali, the Indian festival of lights, my family would visit our Indian neighbours to celebrate the festival with them. My Indian classmate, Devaki, would always let me borrow her traditional Indian costume for the visit. My neighbours were a very strict vegetarian family and I remember helping them light the incense sticks in their prayer room, after which, the whole house would smell of jasmine. During these visits, they would offer us dosa, curries, *muruku* and lots of Indian desserts. Sometimes, we would also get to eat biryani that was specially prepared for their son who lived in Penang and would visit every month.

Back then, my family celebrated every festival and celebration. We enjoyed Christmas, Easter, Good Friday, Vesak Day and Thaipusam. Due to the diversity of cultures in Malaysia, all these celebrations and festivals are public holidays. In fact, Malaysia boasts one of the highest numbers of public holidays in the world.

A Way of Life

Although there are many ethnicities in Malaysia, we are all united as Malaysians. And Malaysians are passionate about food. It is something that connects us and it is our way of showing our hospitality. We would never let guests leave our home without first having had something to eat.

Traditionally, Malays would sit on colourful hand-woven mats on the floor and eat with their hands. Although I have been living abroad for almost 20 years now, I still prefer to eat with my hands. My husband always teases me about it, but it is just my way of appreciating food. To me, it is still the best way to enjoy and savour the flavours of my food.

Like the Malays, Indians eat with their hands as well. Food may even be served on banana leaves.

The Chinese, on the other hand, use chopsticks. I used to watch in awe at how my Chinese friends could pick up single grains of rice using chopsticks! It has taken me years to be able to eat using chopsticks, and I am still not very good at it.

Another thing that ties us together is our staple food — rice. Malaysians eat rice for breakfast, lunch and dinner. One rice dish that is enjoyed at any time of the day is *nasi lemak* (page 20). The rice is cooked using coconut milk, making it very fragrant. It is served with sambal, fried eggs, fried anchovies, fried peanuts and slices of cucumber. This is one of the most well known national dishes of Malaysia.

Top: A typical wooden kampung house in Pekan, the Royal City of Pahang. *Above:* Some members of my family outside their kampung house in Pekan. *Facing page, top:* My girls and I cook together whenever we get the chance to. *Facing page, bottom:* Making curry puffs with Fatimah and Nafeesa, my partners in Malaysian Kitchen UK.

Putting a Meal Together

As with most Asian cuisine, meals are not served in courses. All the dishes prepared for the meal are served at once, to be enjoyed together with rice. As such, I have categorised my recipes by food type to enable you to choose, for example, a meat, a fish and one or two salads or vegetable dishes to make up your meal.

Malaysians don't generally have dessert after meals, although we might have some fruit to cleanse the palette. Instead, we have selections of *kuih muih*, or snacks, that are usually enjoyed in the afternoon with tea. I have included some of my favourites in this collection.

I hope these recipes go some way towards giving you a glimpse of Malaysian cuisine and the dishes that I hold dear to my heart.

Basic Recipes

DRIED CHILLI PASTE
Cili Boh

Makes about 600 g (1 lb 5¹/₃ oz) uncooked chilli paste

150 g (5¹/₃ oz) dried chillies
2 tsp salt

To Cook the Chilli Paste
125 ml (4 fl oz / ¹/₂ cup)
  vegetable oil (optional)
125 ml (4 fl oz / ¹/₂ cup) water
  (optional)

- Cut the chillies lengthwise and remove the seeds. Place in a pot of water and boil until soft. Drain and rinse well, then place in a food processor with the salt and blend to a smooth purée without adding any water. Store in an airtight container. This dried chilli paste will keep for up to a few days in the refrigerator or several months in the freezer.

- Sometimes I go a step further by cooking the paste. To do this, heat the oil in a heavy-bottom pan over medium heat and add the blended chilli. Rinse the food processor with the water and add it to the pan. Bring to a boil, then turn down the heat and let it simmer for 30–45 minutes or until the oil separates.

- Turn off the heat and let it cool completely before transferring to airtight containers. Store in the freezer for use as needed. By cooking the paste, you can reduce your sambal cooking time considerably!

TOASTED GRATED COCONUT
Kerisik

Makes about 1 cup

Using freshly grated coconut
200 g (7 oz) freshly grated
  coconut

Using desiccated coconut
400 g (14¹/₃ oz) desiccated
  coconut
3–4 Tbsp vegetable oil

- This is typically made using freshly grated coconut where it is available, but desiccated coconut makes an acceptable substitute. If using the latter, you will need to toast it with 3–4 Tbsp vegetable oil.

- Heat a non-stick pan over medium heat. Add the coconut (and oil, if using desiccated coconut) and stir continuously with a wooden spoon for 10–12 minutes, until the coconut turns golden brown.

- Use a mortar and pestle to pound the toasted coconut until it turns into a dark, oily and coarse paste.

- The toasted grated coconut can be used immediately. Store any excess in an airtight jar. It will keep for several months. I usually make a big batch and store it in the freezer.

TIP Pound the toasted coconut while it is hot. This will help to get the oil out of the coconut.

PANDAN WATER

Makes about 125 ml (4 fl oz / ¹/₂ cup)

10 pandan leaves
125 ml (4 fl oz / ¹/₂ cup) water

- Rinse the pandan leaves and trim the root ends. Cut the leaves into smaller pieces to fit into your blender.

- Place the leaves in the blender and add the water. Process until the leaves are finely blended and the water is green. Strain the pandan juice using a fine strainer or cheesecloth. Use as needed.

RICE

Makes about 4 cups

2 cups basmati rice
500 ml (16 fl oz / 2 cups)
  water
¹/₂ tsp vegetable oil

- Rinse the rice several times. Drain and place in a heavy-bottom non-stick pan. Add the water and oil.

- Bring to a boil, then simmer, uncovered, for 5 minutes. Cover the pan and turn the heat down to the lowest setting to let the rice dry. This will take another 3–5 minutes. Serve hot.

- Alternatively, cook using a rice cooker.

TIP Adding oil helps prevent the rice from sticking to the bottom of the pot. If you plan to make fried rice, cook the rice a day ahead and store in the fridge to chill it and dry out any excess moisture. This will help the oil coat the grains and the rice will not clump together when frying.

TAMARIND JUICE

Makes about 5 Tbsp

50 g (1³/₄ oz) tamarind pulp
4 Tbsp boiling water

- Place the tamarind pulp in a glass bowl with the boiling water. Let the tamarind soak for 10 minutes until it is soft and mushy.

- Stir the mixture, then strain through a sieve, pushing the pulp through the sieve with a wooden spoon. Discard any bits left in the sieve.

- The juice can be used immediately. Any excess can be stored in the refrigerator for up to a few days.

Rice
and
Noodles

NASI LEMAK
Coconut Rice

Serves 4

370 g (13 oz) basmati rice

2 star anise

2.5-cm (1-inch) length
cinnamon stick

2.5-cm (1-inch) knob ginger,
peeled and thinly sliced
or crushed

2 pandan leaves, rinsed and
tied into a knot

800 ml (26 fl oz / 3¹/₄ cups)
coconut milk

1 tsp salt

1 Tbsp vegetable oil

This coconut-flavoured rice forms the base of Malaysia's most iconic dish, *nasi lemak*. I served *nasi lemak* during the Quarter Finals of my MasterChef UK journey as this dish holds a very special place in my heart, and brings back so many fond memories of my childhood. This fragrant rice can be served plain with *nasi lemak* sambal (page 141), or with side dishes such as rendang (pages 66, 80, 82 or 84) or fried chicken (page 76).

- Rinse the rice and drain. Place in a rice cooker with the rest of the ingredients. Stir to mix, then turn on the rice cooker.

- Alternatively, cook the rice in a non-stick pan. Combine all the ingredients in the pan and place on a stove over medium heat. Cover the pan and let it simmer until the rice is done.

A typical *nasi lemak* spread. Anticlockwise from top: Coconut rice, *nasi lemak* sambal, sliced cucumbers, chicken rendang, hard-boiled eggs, fried anchovies and fried peanuts.

PULUT KUNING
Festive Sticky Rice

Serves 4–6

370 g (13 oz) glutinous rice

2 slices *asam gelugor*

2 tsp turmeric powder

300 ml (10 fl oz / 1¼ cups) coconut milk

A pinch of salt

This rice dish is traditionally served during celebrations such as engagements, weddings, graduations and birthdays. In Malay custom, yellow is associated with royalty, hence this is popularly served at weddings, as the couple getting married is considered king and queen for the day.

....

- Rinse the glutinous rice and drain. Place in a large bowl with the *asam gelugor* and turmeric powder. Add sufficient water to cover the rice and let it soak for 2 hours. Drain the rice using a sieve and set aside.

- Fill a steamer with water and bring to a rolling boil. Place the rice in the steamer and steam for 20 minutes.

- Transfer the rice to a clean bowl.

- Mix the coconut milk with a pinch of salt, then stir it gently into the steamed rice.

- Place the rice back into the steamer and steam for another 20 minutes.

- Transfer the rice back to the bowl and use a wooden spoon to stir the rice gently for a few minutes until it is shiny and compact. This is the effect of the fat from the coconut milk soaking into the rice.

- Serve with a rendang or chicken curry.

NASI MINYAK
Ghee Rice

Serves 4

370 g (13 oz) basmati rice

3 Tbsp ghee (clarified butter)

2 pandan leaves, rinsed and cut into 10-cm (4-inch) lengths

800 ml (26 fl oz / 3¼ cups) water, mixed with 4 Tbsp fresh milk

1 tsp salt

Whole Spices

2.5-cm (1-inch) length cinnamon stick

2 star anise

3 cardamom pods

3 cloves

Spice Paste

2 shallots, peeled

2 cloves garlic, peeled

5-cm (2-inch) knob ginger, peeled

Garnishing (Optional)

A handful of roasted cashew nuts

A handful of dried cranberries

1 Tbsp crisp-fried shallots

A handful of coriander leaves

Colouring (Optional)

A pinch of orange food colouring powder

A pinch of yellow food colouring powder

2 tsp water

Basmati rice is considered to be one of the finest and most flavourful grains. I often use basmati rice to make *nasi minyak* and serve it with curries and pickles on weekends or when we have guests. When making this dish, food colouring is usually added to enhance the look of the dish.

....

- Rinse the rice and drain. Set aside.

- Pound the ingredients for the spice paste coarsely using a mortar and pestle. Set aside.

- Heat the ghee in a heavy-bottom pan over medium heat. Add the whole spices and fry for a few seconds until fragrant.

- Add the spice paste and pandan leaves and fry for 2 minutes until the mixture is slightly dry and fragrant.

- Add the water and milk mixture and salt. Bring to a boil.

- Add the rice and stir gently to mix. Turn the heat down and let it simmer until all the liquid has been evaporated or absorbed. Alternatively, cook the rice using a rice cooker.

- At this point, you can add some colour to the rice, if desired. Mix the orange and yellow food colouring powders separately with 1 tsp water. Sprinkle over the cooked rice and let it sit until you are ready to serve.

- Stir the rice to mix the coloured grains. Dish out and garnish with cashew nuts, cranberries, crisp-fried shallots and/or chopped coriander leaves. Serve hot.

NASI TOMATO
Tomato Rice

Serves 4

370 g (13 oz) basmati rice

3 Tbsp ghee (clarified butter)

1 pandan leaf, rinsed and cut into short lengths

2 Tbsp tomato purée

720 ml (24 fl oz / 2 ⁴/₅ cups) water, mixed with 4 Tbsp fresh milk

Salt, to taste

Whole Spices

2 cloves

5-cm (2-inch) length cinnamon stick

1 star anise

2 cardamom pods

Spice Paste

2 shallots, peeled

1 clove garlic, peeled

5-cm (2-inch) knob ginger, peeled

Garnishing

A handful of roasted cashew nuts

A handful of sultanas

A handful of chopped coriander leaves

This was one of my favourites growing up. My mum would cook it quite often for her catering business and I would always sneak a spoonful to eat when she wasn't looking! I just love the balance of flavours in the dish and since it has a sweet note, it is perfect served with something spicy! I served this in the second round of MasterChef UK with *gulai* Pahang (page 70), a traditional dish from my home state. At that time, I was in a state of panic. I forgot to cook the rice, so I was a little over the time limit when I finally did, but thankfully, the judges said they loved the dish and would wait in line to eat it! Hearing those comments made me feel on top of the world!

- Rinse the rice and drain. Set aside.

- Pound the ingredients for the spice paste coarsely using a mortar and pestle. Set aside.

- Heat the ghee in a medium pot over medium heat. Add the cashew nuts for the garnishing and fry lightly. Remove the cashew nuts and set aside. Add the whole spices and fry until fragrant. Add the pandan leaves and stir.

- Add in the spice paste and the tomato purée. Stir to mix, then add the water and milk mixture. Bring to a boil and season with salt.

- Place the rice in a rice cooker together with the contents of the pot. Turn on the rice cooker to cook the rice.

- Dish out and garnish with cashew nuts, sultanas and coriander leaves. Serve hot.

NASI GORENG KAMPUNG
Kampung-style Fried Rice

Serves 4

4 Tbsp vegetable oil

A handful of dried anchovies

30 g (1 oz) carrot, peeled and diced

45 g (1½ oz) French beans, sliced

3 cups cooked rice, cooled

1 tsp butter

2 eggs

1 Tbsp light soy sauce

A dash of sweet soy sauce

1 green chilli, sliced

Spice Paste

2 cloves garlic, peeled

5 shallots, peeled

1 Tbsp dried shrimps, soaked for 10 minutes to soften

2 red chillies

2 bird's eye chillies

This is the best way to make use of leftover rice. At home, we eat rice daily, and there are always leftovers. I keep the leftovers in the freezer and combine it to make fried rice once every two weeks. This is also a good way to use up any vegetables in the fridge before the next grocery shopping trip. There is no right or wrong in making fried rice. You can add any vegetable you fancy and it will turn out to be a fantastic all-in-one-wok meal.

- Heat the oil in a small frying pan over medium heat. Add the dried anchovies and fry until brown and crisp. Remove and drain well on paper towels. Set aside.

- Place all the ingredients for the spice paste in a blender and process into a coarse paste.

- Transfer the oil used for frying the dried anchovies to a large wok. Heat over medium heat. Add the spice paste and fry until fragrant and the oil separates. This will take about 5 minutes.

- Add the carrot and French beans. Fry for 1 minute.

- Add the rice and stir until the ingredients are well-mixed.

- Push the rice to the side of the wok and add the butter. Crack the eggs into the wok and add the soy sauces. Stir quickly to scramble the eggs, then push the rice back into the middle of the wok. Keep stirring for about 2 minutes until the ingredients are well-mixed.

- Dish out and sprinkle the fried anchovies over the rice. Garnish with sliced green chilli and serve immediately.

NASI GORENG UDANG
Prawn Fried Rice

Serves 4

1 tsp + 3 Tbsp vegetable oil

2 eggs, beaten

3 long beans or French beans, diced

200 g (7 oz) prawns, peeled and deveined, leaving tails intact

3 dried shiitake mushrooms, soaked in hot water to rehydrate, stems removed, caps diced

3 cups cooked rice, cooled

Chilli Paste

3 shallots, peeled and coarsely chopped

2 cloves garlic, peeled and coarsely chopped

5 dried chillies, seeds removed and soaked in hot water to rehydrate, then squeezed to remove excess water before using

Seasoning

1 Tbsp light soy sauce

1 Tbsp oyster sauce

$1/4$ tsp white pepper powder

Salt, to taste

A dash of sesame oil

Garnishing

A handful of chopped spring onions

1 Tbsp crisp-fried shallots

This is my younger daughter's favourite dish, but she loves anything with prawns, really. Besides pizza, *nasi goreng* is our family's favourite food to serve on Friday nights, simply because it is an all-in-one dish that we can enjoy while watching a movie at home. With fried rice, you have the freedom to choose and add vegetables and/or proteins. You can also make use of any leftover vegetables from the fridge. Season it with a simple mix of soy sauce, salt and sliced chilli, and everyone will be coming back for seconds.

....

- Pound the ingredients for the chilli paste coarsely using a mortar and pestle. Set aside.

- Mix the ingredients for the seasoning in a small bowl. Set aside.

- Heat 1 tsp oil in a large frying pan over medium heat. Add the eggs and swirl to coat the entire pan. Let it set, then flip the omelette to cook briefly on the other side. Transfer to a clean dish. Set aside to cool before rolling up and slicing into long strips.

- Heat 3 Tbsp oil in a large wok over medium heat. Add the pounded chilli paste and fry until fragrant and slightly dry.

- Add the diced long/French beans and cook for 2 minutes. Add the prawns and mushrooms and stir-fry for 1–2 minutes.

- Add the seasoning and cooked rice. Fry until the rice is well-mixed with all the ingredients. Taste and adjust the seasoning, if needed.

- Dish out and garnish with the egg strips, chopped spring onions and crisp-fried shallots. Serve immediately.

MEE HOON GORENG MAK
Mum's Fried Rice Vermicelli

Serves 4

150 g (5⅓ oz) dried rice
  vermicelli

1 tsp + 4 Tbsp vegetable oil

2 eggs, lightly beaten (omit if
  making vegetarian noodles)

1 large carrot, peeled and
  cut into fine matchsticks

1 medium white onion,
  peeled and sliced

100 g (3½ oz) bean sprouts,
  tailed

Spice Paste

4 cloves garlic, peeled

4 shallots, peeled

3 Tbsp dried chilli paste
  (page 16)

1 tsp dried shrimps (omit if
  making vegetarian noodles)

4 Tbsp water

Seasoning

1 Tbsp oyster sauce (omit if
  making vegetarian noodles)

1 Tbsp sweet soy sauce

2 tsp light soy sauce

½ tsp sesame oil

1 tsp dark soy sauce

1 Tbsp ketchup

1 Tbsp white vinegar

Garnishing

A handful of fried firm tofu
  slices

Chopped spring onions

This is a firm favourite amongst Malaysians. It is a dish that we enjoy eating for breakfast, lunch and dinner! This dish can be as basic or as lavish as you want. Improvise by adding different vegetables, prawns and chicken. This version is my mother's special version that she would always prepare whenever we went home to visit.

....

- Soak the rice vermicelli in a large bowl of water for about 1 hour. Drain before using.

- Place all the ingredients for the spice paste in a blender and process until fine. Set aside.

- Mix the ingredients for the seasoning in a small bowl. Set aside.

- Heat 1 tsp oil in a large frying pan over medium heat. Add the eggs and swirl to coat the entire pan. Let it set, then flip the omelette to cook briefly on the other side. Transfer to a clean dish. Set aside to cool before rolling up and slicing into long strips.

- Heat 4 Tbsp oil in a large wok over medium heat. Add the blended spice paste and fry until fragrant and the oil starts to separate. This will take about 10 minutes.

- Add the seasoning and stir to combine. Add some water if the mixture gets too dry.

- Add the carrot and onion, and mix well. Add the noodles and bean sprouts and turn the heat to low.

- Using 2 wooden spatulas, lift and turn the noodles until softened and evenly coated with the seasoning. The noodles will continue to soften as it cooks. Stir gently so the noodles don't break.

- Add the egg strips and mix well. You can also serve the eggs on the side.

- Dish out and garnish with fried firm tofu slices and chopped spring onions. Serve immediately.

MEE GORENG MAMAK
Mamak-style Fried Noodles

Serves 4

2 cloves garlic, peeled
   and minced

1 medium white onion,
   peeled and sliced

6 fried tofu puffs, cut into
   bite-sized pieces

2 stalks bok choy, stalks
   and leaves separated

300 g (11 oz) fresh yellow
   noodles

2 eggs

A handful of bean sprouts,
   tailed

Spice Paste
2 tsp curry powder

1 Tbsp sweet soy sauce

1 tsp light soy sauce

1 Tbsp dried chilli paste
   (page 16)

1 Tbsp ketchup

1/2 tsp sugar

A pinch of salt

Fritters
70 g (2 1/2 oz) plain flour

70 g (2 1/2 oz) rice flour

3 Tbsp cornflour

1/2 tsp instant dry yeast

1/2 tsp baking powder

A pinch of sugar

A pinch of salt

180–250 ml (6 fl oz–8 fl oz /
   3/4–1 cup) water

250 ml (8 fl oz / 1 cup)
   vegetable oil

Garnish
1 Tbsp crisp-fried shallots

Sliced green chillies

My all-time favourite dish at *mamak* stalls. *Mamak* stalls are run by Indian-Muslims and you'll find them scattered all over Malaysia. These are the best fried noodles and a trip to Malaysia will not be complete without eating breakfast at one of these stalls. These egg noodles are known for their charred taste and are best eaten with a spicy chilli sambal on the side, accompanied with a large cup of pulled sweet milk tea (*teh tarik*).

....

- Combine the ingredients for the spice paste in a small bowl. Set aside.

- Combine the ingredients for the fritters, except the water and oil, in a bowl. Add water gradually, mixing to get a lumpy batter. Set the batter aside for 15–20 minutes for the yeast and baking powder to work. Heat the oil in a small wok. Add small spoonfuls of the batter to the hot oil and fry until golden brown. Remove and drain well. Set aside to cool before cutting into bite-sized pieces.

- Use the same wok and discard all but 2 Tbsp oil. Reheat the oil over low heat. Add the garlic and onion and fry until fragrant.

- Add the spice paste and fry for 2 minutes.

- Add the fried tofu puffs, fritters and bok choy stalks. Stir and let it cook for another minute.

- Add the noodles and stir to mix, then push the noodles to the side of the wok. Crack in the eggs and quickly scramble them. Bring the noodles back into the centre of the wok and mix with the eggs.

- Add the bok choy leaves and bean sprouts. Stir-fry for about 1 minute until the ingredients are well-mixed and the noodles are very dry.

- Dish out and garnish with crisp-fried shallots and green chillies. Serve immediately.

MEE CALONG
Fish Ball Noodles

Serves 4

1 packet Chinese egg
  noodles or rice vermicelli

3 stalks bok choy

1 Tbsp vegetable oil

1 litre (32 fl oz / 4 cups)
  water

1 fish stock cube

Salt, to taste

Fish Balls

250 g (9 oz) Spanish
  mackerel

$1/2$ tsp white pepper powder

1 Tbsp cornflour

1 egg white (optional)

1 tsp salt

Spice Paste

5 shallots, peeled

2 cloves garlic, peeled

1 tsp black peppercorns

Chilli Soy Sauce

10 bird's eye chillies,
  thinly sliced

1 clove garlic, peeled
  and minced

2 Tbsp sweet soy sauce

1 Tbsp white vinegar

1 tsp salt

Topping

3 red chillies, sliced

A handful of chopped
  coriander leaves

1 Tbsp crisp-fried shallots

This dish is very popular in the East Coast of Malaysia. Being near to the coast, there is an abundant supply of seafood, and the fish balls you get here are as fresh as you can get them!

- Boil a pot of water and blanch the noodles and bok choy lightly. Drain and divide among 4 serving bowls.

- Place all the ingredients for the fish balls into a food processor and process into a paste. Form into small balls and set aside.

- Place all the ingredients for the spice paste into a clean blender and process until fine. Set aside.

- Place all the ingredients for the chilli soy sauce in a clean blender and process until fine. Set aside.

- Heat the oil in a large pot over medium heat. Add the blended spice paste and fry until fragrant.

- Add the water and bring to a boil. Add the fish stock cube and salt. Turn down the heat and let it simmer for 10 minutes.

- Add the fish balls and stir gently. The fish balls are done when they float.

- Ladle the hot soup with some fish balls into each serving bowl with the noodles and bok choy. Garnish with chillies, coriander leaves and crisp-fried shallots. Add chilli soy sauce to taste. Serve immediately.

MEE HOON SUP BEREMPAH
Spiced Rice Noodle Soup

Serves 4

This dish is very similar to the Indonesian *mee soto*. There are many variations of this dish and this is what our family likes to eat, a spiced broth topped with fiery blended chillies with a side of comforting potato cutlets. It's the perfect winter comfort food!

Vegetable oil, as needed

500 g (1 lb 1½ oz) chicken breast

2 litres (64 fl oz / 8 cups) water

1 chicken stock cube

200 g (7 oz) dried rice vermicelli

A handful of bean sprouts

A handful of Chinese celery

1 Tbsp crisp-fried shallots

Potato Cutlets
300 g (11 oz) potatoes

50 g (1¾ oz) chicken meat

2 tsp minced garlic

4 Tbsp chopped spring onions

4 Tbsp chopped coriander leaves

2 Tbsp crisp-fried shallots

1 egg yolk

¼ tsp white pepper powder

2 tsp cornflour

A pinch of salt

1 egg white

Spice Paste
2 Tbsp coriander powder

2 tsp cumin powder

2 tsp fennel powder

1 tsp white pepper powder

½ tsp black pepper powder

4 Tbsp water

4 shallots, peeled

2 cloves garlic, peeled

5-cm (2-inch) knob ginger, peeled

Tempering Spices
4 cloves

3 cardamom pods

1 stalk lemongrass, white part only, bruised

2 star anise

2.5-cm (1-inch) length cinnamon stick

Spicy Chilli Vinegar
5 red chillies

3 bird's eye chillies

2 shallots, peeled

1–2 Tbsp white vinegar

Salt, to taste

Sugar, to taste

- Prepare the potato cutlets. Boil the potatoes until tender, then peel and place in a large bowl. Boil to cook the chicken, then pound using a mortar and pestle. Place in the bowl with the potatoes. Add the remaining ingredients, except the egg white, and mash. Form the mixture into 2.5-cm (1-inch) balls and flatten slightly. Set aside.

- Place the ingredients for the spice paste in a blender and process until smooth.

- Heat 2 Tbsp oil in a large pot over medium heat. Add the tempering spices and fry until it starts to splutter. Add the spice paste and turn down the heat. Cook until the oil separates.

- Add the chicken breast, water and stock cube. Bring to a boil, then turn down the heat and let it simmer for 30 minutes.

- Remove the chicken breast and set aside to cool before shredding. Cover and set aside. Check the soup for seasoning and keep hot.

- In another wok, heat sufficient oil for deep-frying over medium heat. Dip the potato cutlets in egg white and lower into the hot oil. Do this in small batches. Deep-fry for 1 minute on each side until golden brown. Remove and drain well on paper towels. Set aside.

- Place all the ingredients for the spicy chilli vinegar in a blender and process for 30 seconds. Transfer to a clean bowl.

- To serve, boil a pot of water and blanch the noodles. Drain and divide among 4 serving bowls. Top with shredded chicken, bean sprouts and Chinese celery. Spoon the hot soup over and garnish with crisp-fried shallots. Top with the potato cutlets and serve the spicy chilli vinegar on the side.

LAKSAM
Rolled Noodles in Black Pepper Gravy

Serves 6

Rolled Noodles

420 g (15 oz) rice flour

70 g (2 1/2 oz) plain flour

1.25 litres (40 fl oz / 5 cups) warm water

2 tsp salt

2 Tbsp vegetable oil

Gravy

250 ml (8 fl oz / 1 cup) water

1 tsp salt

500 g (1 lb 1 1/2 oz) Spanish mackerel

500 ml (16 fl oz / 2 cups) coconut milk

1 Tbsp sugar

1/2 tsp salt

2 slices *asam gelugor*

Spices

4 shallots, peeled

1 clove garlic, peeled

1 tsp grated ginger

1 tsp black peppercorns

Topping

A handful of bean sprouts, tailed

5 long beans, finely chopped

1/2 medium cucumber, shredded

Laksa leaves, thinly sliced (optional)

1 torch ginger bud, thinly sliced

Chilli Paste

10 dried chillies, seeds removed and soaked in hot water to rehydrate, then squeezed to remove excess water before using

2.5-cm (1-inch) fermented prawn paste, toasted

1/2 tsp salt

This recipe is lengthy, but I promise the result is well worth the effort! *Laksam* is unlike other noodle soups, as it is served in a creamy black pepper sauce and topped with a variety of vegetables and a chilli paste. I love making this dish, especially the rolled noodles, since it reminds me of my childhood when I would watch with fascination as the laksa vendor made this at her stall near our house.

- Place all the ingredients for the noodles in a mixing bowl and stir using a whisk, making sure there are no lumps.

- Prepare a steamer and a baking tray that will fit into the steamer.

- Coat the tray well with oil. Pour a little rice flour mixture into the prepared tray to form a thin layer (*see* Note). Place into the steamer and steam for about 5 minutes. Remove the tray and run a small spatula along the edges of the rice flour sheet to loosen it, then roll it up, making sure it doesn't break. Rub some oil on the roll and place on a clean plate. Cover with cling film and set aside.

- Repeat the step above until the mixture is used up.

- Prepare the gravy. Boil the water in a small pot. Add the salt and fish, and poach until the fish is cooked through. Remove the fish and debone. Strain the poaching stock and set aside.

- Place the fish into a food processor. Add the spices and poaching stock, and blend into a paste. Transfer to a medium pot. Add the coconut milk, sugar, salt and *asam gelugor* and bring to a boil. Turn down the heat to low and simmer for 20 minutes.

- Taste and adjust the seasoning, if needed. Add more water if the gravy is too thick, but be careful not to add too much water since the gravy needs to coat the noodles when you eat it.

- Pound the ingredients for the chilli paste coarsely using a mortar and pestle. Set aside.

- To serve, cut the noodle logs into bite-sized pieces. Place into bowls and spoon the gravy over. Add the topping and chilli paste. Enjoy!

NOTE I use a 23-cm (9-inch) round pizza pan when I make this and add half a cup of rice flour mixture per noodle log. This will depend on the size of your steamer and pan, but the rule of thumb is that the mixture should be no thicker than 0.5-cm (1/4-in).

I get the fishmonger to fillet the fish for me. At home, I boil the fish and bones separately. This saves a lot of time.

ROTI JALA
Lace Crepes

Makes about 21 crepes

200 g (7 oz) plain flour

1 large egg, at room temperature

200 ml (6¾ fl oz) water

150 ml (5 fl oz) milk

3 Tbsp vegetable oil

A pinch of salt

A pinch of turmeric powder

Roti jala, also known as lace crepes or net pancakes, is one of the most requested menu items for my cookery lessons and food demos in the UK. The recipe is very similar to basic French crepes, except that it uses fewer eggs. A pinch of turmeric powder is also added for colour. To create the lacy pattern, I use a squeeze sauce bottle with three nozzles. A single nozzle works as well, and you can use your imagination to create any design. In Malaysia, *roti jala* makers are used. These are basically cups with three to five spouts. Some home cooks may also use their fingers to drizzle the batter. Whichever way these delicious crepes are made, they are best enjoyed with creamy chicken curry.

....

- Place all the ingredients in a blender and process. Pour the resulting batter through a sieve into a jug to remove any lumps of flour. Transfer the batter into a squeeze sauce bottle and set aside for 20 minutes.

- Heat a non-stick pan over medium heat. Squeeze the batter onto the pan while moving your hand in a circular motion to form a lacy design about 15 cm (6 inches) in diameter. I make mine with a squarish net design.

- Leave to cook for 1 minute. Cook the crepe only on one side, so the other side remains glossy. Transfer to a plate.

- Fold the left and right sides of the crepe towards the centre, then roll it up tightly like a spring roll. Repeat with the remaining ingredients.

- Serve with a chicken curry.

NOTE To make these crepes vegan, omit the eggs and use coconut milk in place of milk.

 RiceandNoodles

Fish and Seafood

IKAN MASAK ASAM
Fish in Tamarind Sauce

Serves 4

1 sea bream, sea bass or
  red mullet, gutted and
  cleaned

1/2 tsp salt

2 tsp turmeric powder

250 ml (8 fl oz / 1 cup)
  vegetable oil

3 shallots, peeled and thinly
  sliced

3 cloves garlic, peeled and
  cut into thin slices

2.5-cm (1-inch) knob ginger,
  peeled and cut into thin
  strips

2–3 Tbsp tamarind juice
  (page 17)

1 tsp sugar

1 Tbsp oyster sauce

1 green chilli, cut into thin
  strips

1 red chilli, cut into thin strips

4 bird's eye chillies, bruised

125 ml (4 fl oz / 1/2 cup) water

2 medium white onions,
  peeled and sliced

Cooking this dish is my sister-in-law, Rokiah's speciality, and this is her recipe for which I have her full blessing and permission to share. I love how such simple ingredients contribute to making this super delicious dish. You can use boneless fish fillet instead of a whole fish. Simply cut the fillet into small pieces and follow the method from step 2.

· ·

- Score the fish on both sides.

- Rub the fish with salt and turmeric powder and set aside for 10 minutes.

- Heat the oil in a non-stick wok over medium heat. Gently lower the fish into the hot oil and fry until crispy. Remove and drain on paper towels. Arrange on a serving plate and keep warm.

- Using a clean wok, reheat 2 Tbsp oil over medium heat. Add the shallots, garlic and ginger and fry gently until it starts to brown.

- Add the tamarind juice, sugar, oyster sauce and chillies. Stir for a few minutes, then add the water and bring to a boil.

- Add the onions, then pour the sauce over the fried fish. Serve immediately with rice and other dishes on the side.

IKAN SINGGANG
East Coast Fish Broth

Serves 4

1 litre (32 fl oz / 4 cups)
  water

3 slices *asam gelugor*

1 fish stock cube

2 bird's eye chillies,
  or to taste

2.5-cm (1-inch) knob
  galangal, peeled

1/4 tsp turmeric powder

1 clove garlic, peeled

4 Spanish mackerel steaks
  or other preferred fish,
  total about 300 g (11 oz)

Salt, to taste

This fish broth is a favourite among the Malays living along the
East Coast of Malaysia. The simplicity of this dish belies the explosion
of flavours that will hit you especially if you bite into the bird's eye chillies.
There's not much to this recipe and I highly recommend that you try this
at least once. Sometimes, easy dishes are the most tasty.

- Bring the water to a boil in a small pot. Add the *asam gelugor*, fish
  stock cube, bird's eye chillies, galangal, turmeric powder and garlic.

- Let the water return to the boil, then turn the heat to medium and
  simmer for 20 minutes.

- Add the fish and simmer for another 5 minutes until the fish is cooked
  through.

- Taste and adjust the seasoning, if needed. The soup should have an
  intense sour and salty flavour.

- Serve hot with rice.

KARI IKAN MAK
Mum's Fish Curry

Serves 4

4 basa fillets or whole
  Spanish mackerel, gutted
  and cleaned, total about
  300 g (11 oz)

3 Tbsp vegetable oil

1 stalk curry leaves, stem
  discarded

4 cloves garlic, peeled and
  sliced

3 shallots, peeled and sliced

2.5-cm (1-inch) knob ginger,
  peeled and sliced

500 ml (16 fl oz / 2 cups)
  coconut milk

4 Tbsp tamarind juice, or to
  taste (page 17)

1 tsp salt, or to taste

3 tomatoes, cut into quarters

8 ladies' fingers, ends
  trimmed

Tempering Spices

1 tsp fenugreek

$^1/_2$ tsp mustard seeds

$^1/_2$ tsp fennel seeds

$^1/_2$ tsp cumin seeds

Spice Paste

2 Tbsp curry powder

1 Tbsp chilli powder,
  or to taste

1 tsp turmeric powder

125 ml (4 fl oz / $^1/_2$ cup) water

I cook this often for my family, and if I could, I would cook it every day!
I adapted this dish from my mum's recipe which is very spicy, as my
younger daughter preferred a creamier sauce. In the UK, I use basa fillet,
but in Malaysia, I would always go for whole Spanish mackerel.

••

- Cut the fish into small pieces. Set aside.

- Heat the oil in a large pot over medium heat. Add the tempering
  spices and curry leaves. Cover with a lid and let the spices splutter.

- Add the garlic, shallots and ginger and fry for about 1 minute until
  fragrant. Turn the heat down.

- Combine the ingredients for the spice paste and add to the pot.
  Stir constantly, so the spice paste does not burn. Add more water
  if it gets too dry. The spice paste is cooked when the oil separates.

- Add the coconut milk, tamarind juice and salt. Let the curry boil
  over medium heat for 10 minutes.

- Add the tomatoes and ladies' fingers. Cook for another 2 minutes,
  until the ladies' fingers are tender.

- Add the fish and simmer for 5 minutes until the fish is cooked through.

- Taste and adjust the seasoning, if needed. Serve hot with rice or bread.

SAMBAL UDANG
Prawn Sambal

Serves 4

300 g (11 oz) king prawns

250 ml (8 fl oz / 1 cup) water

4 Tbsp vegetable oil

1 stalk lemongrass, white
part only, bruised

4 Tbsp tamarind juice
(page 17)

A pinch of salt

2 Tbsp sugar

1 medium white onion,
peeled and sliced

Sambal

8 shallots, peeled

4 fresh red chillies

3 Tbsp dried chilli paste
(page 16)

1 medium white onion,
peeled

1 clove garlic, peeled

1 stalk lemongrass, white
part only, roughly chopped

125 ml (4 fl oz / ½ cup) water

Sambal is the general term for spicy chilli-based pastes that are popular all over South East Asia. It takes time to make sambals, since the process of cooking the chillies is long, but it is well worth the time and trouble. I usually cook a big pot of sambal, pack it into small tubs, label them and place them in the freezer. This way, I do the work once and have a good supply of sambal, especially for those super-busy days when I don't have the time to cook a proper meal. I just need to defrost the sambal on the stove over low heat. And once the oil separates, I can add the other ingredients.

....

- Peel and devein the prawns. Reserve the heads and shells. Rinse the prawns and set aside.

- Place the prawn heads and shells in a pot. Add the water and boil for 10 minutes. This will be the stock for the dish. Strain the stock and discard the heads and shells. Set aside.

- Place the ingredients for the sambal in a blender and process into a paste.

- Heat the oil in a pan over medium heat. Add the sambal paste and stir-fry until fragrant.

- Add the prawn stock and bruised lemongrass. Cook until the oil separates. This will take 20–30 minutes. Keep the heat on medium to low.

- Add the tamarind juice and stir to incorporate. Continue to cook until the sauce is thick like a paste. Add the prawns, then season with salt and sugar. You can now adjust the consistency of the sambal to your preference. For a thinner sambal, add just a little water and mix well.

- Add the onion and stir for about 2 minutes until the prawns are cooked through. The onions will continue to soften in the residual heat.

- Dish out and serve hot with rice and other dishes on the side.

SAMBAL IKAN HIJAU
Fish in Green Sambal

Serves 4

2 whole seabass or
  1 medium red snapper,
  gutted and cleaned

1 tsp turmeric powder

Salt, as needed

125 ml (4 fl oz / 1/2 cup)
  vegetable oil

1 kaffir lime leaf, finely sliced

1 tsp sugar

3–4 white onion rounds

Green Sambal

3 cloves garlic, peeled

5-cm (2-inch) knob ginger,
  peeled

6 shallots, peeled

2 candlenuts

2 tsp coriander powder

4 green chillies

4 green bird's eye chillies

125 ml (4 fl oz / 1/2 cup) water

We moved to Geoje Island, a shipbuilding site in South Korea in 2008. Back then, there were no Asian shops and we had to drive a good few hours to get groceries. We couldn't even get fresh chillies, especially red ones, so I started making sambal using green chillies. After some experimenting, I came up with this green sambal dish. I hope you like it as much as my family does!

....

- Pat the fish dry and score it on both sides.

- Rub the fish with turmeric powder and 1/2 tsp salt. Set aside to marinade for 15 minutes.

- Place the ingredients for the green sambal in a blender and process until fine. Set aside.

- Heat the oil in a non-stick pan over medium heat. Gently lower the fish into the hot oil and fry until brown and crisp on both sides. Remove and drain on paper towels. Set aside.

- Transfer 2 Tbsp oil to a clean non-stick pan over medium heat. Add the green sambal paste and stir-fry until the oil separates.

- Add the kaffir lime leaf, sugar and a pinch of salt. Taste and adjust the seasoning, if needed.

- Add the fried fish and stir gently, making sure the fish is well-coated with the sauce.

- Dish out and garnish with onion rounds. Serve immediately with rice and a stir-fried vegetable dish on the side.

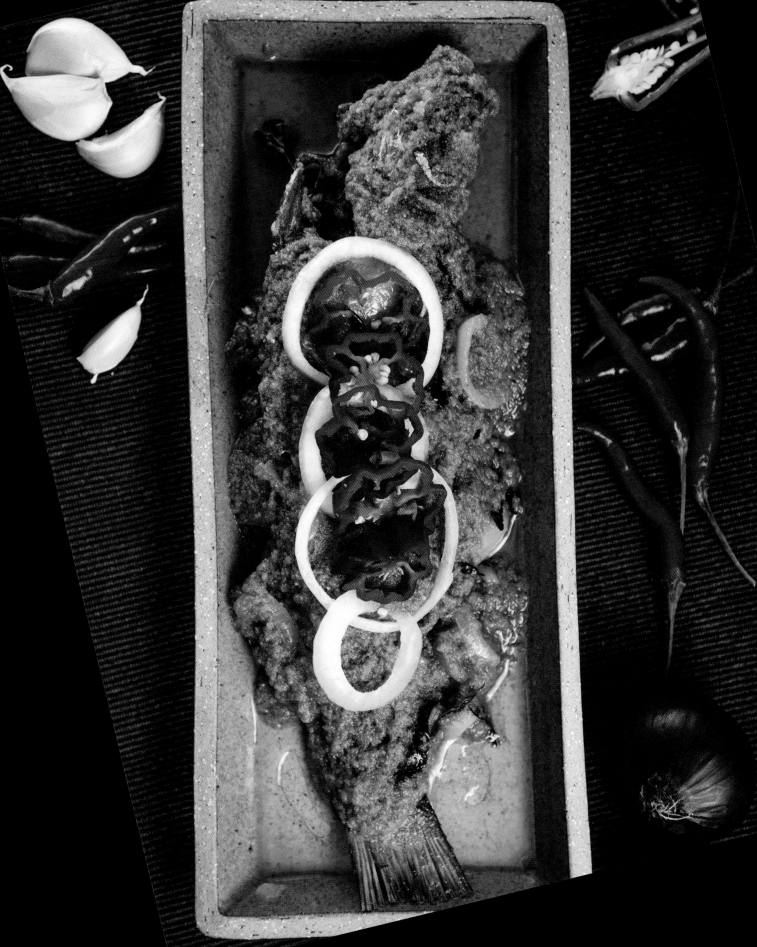

SOTONG SOS TIRAM
Squid in Oyster Sauce

Serves 4–6

300 g (11 oz) squid

1 Tbsp vegetable oil

3 cloves garlic, peeled
and sliced

2 stalks lemongrass, white
part only, bruised

5-cm (2-inch) knob ginger,
peeled and cut into thin
strips

2 Tbsp tamarind juice
(page 17)

4 bird's eye chillies, or
to taste, bruised

2 red chillies, cut into
thin strips

3 Tbsp oyster sauce

1 medium white onion,
peeled and sliced

1 tsp turmeric powder

Salt, to taste

Squid is an exquisite seafood that can be served on its own as a main dish or as an accompaniment, depending on how it is prepared. It can, however, be a bit tricky to get it cooked to the right texture. For this dish, the trick to getting it done just right is to score and blanch the squid, then plunge it into cold water, before adding it to the cooked spice paste. This will ensure that the squid does not overcook and remains tender.

- Prepare the squid. Pull the squid head and tentacles from the body. Cut the tentacles just behind the eyes and discard the innards. Remove the beak from the tentacles. Remove the cuttlebone from the body and discard. Peel away the skin. Rinse the tentacles and body thoroughly.

- Cut open the body and make shallow criss-cross cuts on the inside. Cut into bite-sized pieces.

- Place the squid in a shallow saucepan and add enough water just to cover. Poach for 3 minutes, then remove the squid and quickly plunge into cold water to stop the cooking process. This will prevent the squid from becoming tough and chewy. Discard the poaching liquid.

- Heat the oil in a pan over medium heat. Add the garlic, lemongrass and ginger and stir-fry until fragrant.

- Add the tamarind juice and chillies. Stir-fry for 1 minute.

- Add the oyster sauce and onion and stir until everything is incorporated.

- Add the poached squid and turmeric powder. Mix well and add salt to taste.

- Dish out and serve hot with rice and other dishes.

KETUPAT SOTONG
Malaysian-style Stuffed Squid

Serves 4

4 medium to large squid

Toothpicks, as needed

3 shallots, peeled and thinly sliced

2.5-cm (1-inch) knob ginger, peeled and cut into thin strips

1 tsp fenugreek

1 tsp salt

1 Tbsp sugar

1 tsp Thai fish sauce

500 ml (16 fl oz / 2 cups) coconut milk

Filling

125 ml (4 fl oz / ½ cup) coconut milk

500 ml (16 fl oz / 2 cups) water

185 g (6½ oz) glutinous rice

A pinch of salt

This is another dish that is popular in the East Coast of Malaysia, particularly in the state of Kelantan. As the squid is stuffed with glutinous rice, this dish can be served as a main course with a curry, or *gulai*, and sambal, but it is also often enjoyed as a snack.

....

- Prepare the filling ahead. Combine the coconut milk and water in a large bowl. Add the glutinous rice and salt. Leave to soak for 4 hours.

- Prepare the squid. Pull the squid head and tentacles from the body. Cut the tentacles just behind the eyes and discard the innards. Remove the beak from the tentacles. Remove the cuttlebone from the squid tube and discard. Peel away the skin. Rinse the tentacles and squid tube thoroughly.

- Stuff the soaked rice into the squid tubes and plug the opening with the tentacles. Secure with toothpicks.

- Place the shallots, ginger, fenugreek, salt, sugar and fish sauce into a wide frying pan, then add the coconut milk. Arrange the stuffed squid in a single layer in the frying pan and bring to a boil over medium heat, stirring continuously to prevent the coconut milk from curdling.

- Turn the heat to low and simmer for 30 minutes until the rice is done. Dish out and serve.

IKAN MASAK MASAM MANIS
Sweet and Sour Fish

Serves 4

1 large grouper or sea bass, gutted and cleaned

2 tsp turmeric powder

1 Tbsp cornflour

1 tsp salt

Vegetable oil, as needed

3 cloves garlic, peeled and minced

1 Tbsp minced ginger

40 g (1$^{1}/_{3}$ oz) red capsicum (bell pepper), cored and finely diced

40 g (1$^{1}/_{3}$ oz) carrot, peeled and finely diced

40 g (1$^{1}/_{3}$ oz) cucumber, finely diced

40 g (1$^{1}/_{3}$ oz) pineapple, finely diced

1 medium white onion, peeled and sliced

Sauce

200 ml (6$^{3}/_{4}$ fl oz) water

3 Tbsp ketchup

3 Tbsp sweet chilli sauce

1 Tbsp spicy chilli sauce

1 Tbsp oyster sauce

1–2 Tbsp white vinegar

1–2 Tbsp sugar

$^{1}/_{2}$ tsp sesame oil

1 tsp cornflour

This Malaysian-style sweet and sour dish has a little chilli kick to make it more scrumptious. There are many ways to make this dish and this is my take on it. My elder daughter loves to cook it on weekends.

···

- Score the fish on both sides.

- Rub the fish with turmeric powder, cornflour and salt.

- Heat sufficient oil for deep-frying in a pan over medium heat. Gently lower the fish into the hot oil and deep-fry until crispy.

- Remove the fish and drain well. Arrange on a large serving plate and set aside.

- Combine the ingredients for the sauce in a bowl and mix well. Set aside.

- Transfer 3 Tbsp oil to a clean wok over medium heat. Add the garlic and ginger and stir-fry until fragrant.

- Add the sauce and cook until thickened slightly. Add the diced vegetables and onion and mix well.

- Pour the sauce over the fried fish. Serve immediately with rice and other dishes.

LEMAK CILI PADI UDANG
Prawn and Pineapple Curry

Serves 4

300 g (11 oz) large tiger
prawns

250 ml (8 fl oz / 1 cup) boiling
water

375 ml (12 fl oz / 1½ cups)
thick coconut milk

1 stalk lemongrass, white
part only, bruised

½ tsp turmeric powder

1 slice *asam gelugor*

150 g (5⅓ oz) pineapple,
cut into cubes (optional)

1 turmeric leaf

Salt, to taste

Spice Paste

6 shallots, peeled and
roughly chopped

2 green chillies, roughly
chopped

6 bird's eye chillies, or
to taste

125 ml (4 fl oz / ½ cup) water

This is a traditional Malay recipe from my sister-in-law, Molly. You can substitute the prawns for fish or chicken. Note that if using chicken, it will take a longer time to cook.

....

- Peel and devein the prawns. Reserve the heads and shells. Rinse the prawns and set aside.

- Place the prawn heads and shells in a pot. Add the boiling water and simmer for 15 minutes. This will be the stock for the dish. Strain the stock and discard the heads and shells (see Note).

- Place all the ingredients for the spice paste in a blender and process into a coarse paste.

- Transfer the spice paste to a medium saucepan. Add the stock, coconut milk, lemongrass, turmeric powder and *asam gelugor*. Bring to a boil while stirring continuously to prevent the coconut milk from curdling.

- Add the pineapple and turmeric leaf. Season with salt.

- Add the prawns and stir gently. Turn down the heat and let it simmer for 2 minutes until the prawns are done. Remove from heat.

- Dish out and serve with rice and other dishes.

NOTE I sometimes cook the prawns whole, leaving the heads and shells on, since it is very hard to find large fresh prawns where I am in Bristol. It is also entirely your preference if you like to keep them whole or peeled.

Meat
and
Poultry

RENDANG AYAM MASTERCHEF UK
My "Non Crispy" MasterChef UK Chicken Rendang

Serves 6

1 large chicken, about 1.5 kg
  (3 lb 4¹/₂ oz)

4 Tbsp vegetable oil

1 tsp salt, or to taste

1 slice *asam gelugor*

40 g (1¹/₃ oz) palm sugar,
  or to taste

120 g (4¹/₃ oz) toasted grated
  coconut (page 16)

500 ml (16 fl oz / 2 cups)
  coconut milk

1 tsp turmeric powder

2 turmeric leaves, finely
  sliced

Spice Paste

150 g (5¹/₃ oz) dried chilli
  paste (page 16)

150 g (5¹/₃ oz) shallots, peeled

3 cloves garlic, peeled

2 candlenuts

3 stalks lemongrass, white
  part only, roughly chopped

7.5-cm (3-inch) knob ginger,
  peeled and sliced

7.5-cm (3-inch) knob
  galangal, peeled and sliced

250 ml (8 fl oz / 1 cup)
  coconut milk

Another family favourite that now holds a special place in my heart for a very different reason. This dish used to remind me of my mother, and now it has also given me the opportunity to write this book. I served this rendang together with my *nasi lemak* (page 20), on my last episode on MasterChef UK. The controversy that came with it presented me with so many opportunities…so it was really a blessing in disguise!

....

- Wash the chicken and pat dry. Cut into 10 pieces. Set aside.

- Place all the ingredients for the spice paste in a blender and process until smooth. Add a little water to help the blades move, if needed.

- Heat the oil in a non-stick pan over medium heat. Add the spice paste, salt and *asam gelugor* to get the flavour into the spice. Stir for 2–3 minutes, then turn down the heat and let it simmer for about 20 minutes, or until the oil separates.

- Add the chicken, palm sugar, toasted grated coconut, coconut milk, turmeric powder and turmeric leaves. Let the mixture return to the boil, then turn down the heat. Let it simmer for 20 minutes, or until the oil separates again, the sauce is thick and the chicken is cooked through.

- Taste and adjust the seasoning, if needed. Dish out and serve with rice and other dishes.

NOTE The oil separates twice in this rendang recipe and you will get a wonderful flavour from this double simmering process. Should the rendang become too dry while simmering, add just enough water to keep it from drying up.

In this recipe, turmeric leaves can be replaced with kaffir lime leaves, if they are not available.

AYAM GOLEK
Malaysian-style Roast Chicken

Serves 6

1 small chicken, about 1 kg
  (2 lb 3 oz)

Marinade

6 shallots, peeled

2 cloves garlic, peeled

3 stalks lemongrass, white
  part only, roughly chopped

2 tsp grated ginger

$1/2$ tsp turmeric powder

2 Tbsp dried chilli paste
  (page 16)

7.5-cm (3-inch) knob
  galangal, peeled and sliced

Sauce

2 Tbsp vegetable oil

200 ml ($6^3/_4$ fl oz) coconut milk

A pinch of salt

1–2 tsp sugar

At Malay wedding ceremonies, roast chicken is usually served to the bride and groom as part of their first meal together as husband and wife. In the early days of our marriage, I cooked this dish for my husband, on top of all the other special Eid dishes, to celebrate our life together, and to remind him that Malaysians also have a roast chicken dish! Hence, this dish holds a special place in my heart. This roast is definitely a crowd pleaser and any leftovers are perfect for making cold sandwiches the next day.

- Wash the chicken and pat dry. Set aside.

- Place the ingredients for the marinade in a food processor and process into a fine paste. Do not add any water.

- Rub half the marinade all over the outside of the chicken. Place the remaining half of the marinade in an airtight container and refrigerate until needed.

- Place the chicken on a roasting tray and cover with aluminium foil. Set aside for at least 2 hours, or if time allows, overnight, to allow the flavours to be absorbed.

- When ready to cook, preheat the oven to 180°C (350°F).

- Place the roasting tray with the chicken on the lower rack of the oven. Bake for 1 hour 20 minutes, or until the chicken is cooked through and tender.

- Prepare the sauce. Heat 2 Tbsp oil in a small pot over medium heat. Add the remaining marinade and cook, stirring, for 5 minutes. Add the coconut milk and stir to combine. Taste and adjust the seasoning with salt and sugar, if needed. Stir to mix, then simmer over low heat until the oil separates.

- Pour the sauce over the chicken and place under the grill for 3–5 minutes to brown a little. Arrange on a serving plate and serve.

GULAI PAHANG
Pahang-style Curry

Serves 6

1 small chicken, about 1 kg
  (2 lb 3 oz)

4 Tbsp vegetable oil

1 stalk lemongrass, white
  part only, bruised

7.5-cm (3-inch) knob
  galangal, peeled and thinly
  sliced

2 medium potatoes, peeled
  and cut into quarters

1–2 tsp salt

500 ml (16 fl oz / 2 cups)
  thick coconut milk

100 ml (3 1/2 fl oz) double
  cream

Spice Paste

3 red chillies

5 bird's eye chillies (optional)

5 shallots, peeled

2 cloves garlic, peeled

2 tsp fermented prawn
  paste, toasted

1 Tbsp coriander powder

2 tsp fennel powder

1 tsp cumin powder

1 tsp turmeric powder

3 Tbsp dried chilli paste
  (page 16)

85 ml (2 1/2 fl oz / 1/3 cup)
  water

The Malay word *gulai* can refer to a traditional cooking method or to a dish. I grew up eating this *gulai* prepared by my late mother and I call it *gulai* Pahang in honour of her. To me, she made the best *gulai,* and her secret must be that she used the traditional grinding stone to grind the spices. I prepared and served this dish with *nasi tomato* (page 26) and tangy *acar nenas saffron* (page 92) at the start of my MasterChef UK journey. The positive comments I received for it are a tribute to my wonderful, loving mother.

....

- Wash the chicken and pat dry. Cut into 8 pieces. Set aside.

- Place the ingredients for the spice paste in a blender and process until smooth.

- Heat the oil in a saucepan over medium heat. Add the spice paste and stir-fry until fragrant.

- Add the lemongrass and galangal and stir-fry for 5 minutes. Add a little water if the spice paste becomes too dry. Let it cook for about 10 minutes, or until the oil separates.

- Add the chicken and gently stir to coat the chicken with the paste. Add the potatoes, salt and coconut milk and bring to a boil.

- Turn the heat down and let it simmer until the chicken is cooked through and the potatoes are tender.

- Add the double cream and stir. Taste and adjust the seasoning, if needed. You can add more cream if it is too spicy for your liking.

- Serve hot with rice and other dishes.

AYAM MASAK HITAM
Zen Chicken

Serves 4

450 g (1 lb) chicken breast meat

¹/₂ tsp salt

1 tsp turmeric powder

250 ml (8 fl oz) vegetable oil

1 tsp tamarind juice (page 17)

1 Tbsp honey, or to taste

2 Tbsp ketchup

4 Tbsp sweet soy sauce

5 kaffir lime leaves, thinly sliced

1 medium white onion, peeled and sliced

Spice Paste

8 shallots, peeled

4 cloves garlic, peeled

4 Tbsp dried chilli paste (page 16)

7.5-cm (3-inch) knob ginger, peeled and sliced

2 stalks lemongrass, white part only, roughly chopped

2 candlenuts

1 large white onion, peeled and cut into quarters

250 ml (8 fl oz / 1 cup) water

This is one of our family favourites! Calling it Zen chicken may seem a little odd, but we chose the name to reflect the perfect balance of flavours — sweetness from the honey, tanginess from the ketchup, spiciness from the chillies and a refreshing citrus flavour from the kaffir lime leaves. We enjoy using chicken in this dish, but these flavours are also great with fish, beef or tofu.

....

- Place all the ingredients for the spice paste in a blender and process until fine. Set aside.

- Cut the chicken into strips and coat with salt and turmeric powder. Set aside for 15 minutes.

- Heat the oil in a wok over medium heat. Gently lower the chicken strips into the hot oil and deep-fry until brown and crispy. Do this in batches. Drain well and set aside.

- Leave 3 Tbsp oil in the wok and reheat. Add the spice paste and cook until the oil separates. This will take 20–30 minutes. Add a little water if the paste becomes too dry.

- Add the tamarind juice, honey, ketchup and sweet soy sauce and continue to stir for another 5 minutes. The sauce should be thick and sticky.

- Add kaffir lime leaves and chicken strips. Stir to mix. Taste and adjust the seasoning, if needed.

- Turn up the heat and add the onion. Stir for another minute, so the sauce coats the onion.

- Dish out and serve hot with rice and other dishes.

AYAM MASAK MERAH
Chicken Sambal

Serves 6

1 small chicken, about 1 kg
  (2 lb 3 oz)

4 Tbsp vegetable oil

250 ml (8 fl oz / 1 cup)
  coconut milk

1 Tbsp tamarind juice
  (page 17)

1 tsp salt, or to taste

2 turmeric leaves, finely
  sliced

1 medium white onion,
  peeled and sliced

Spice Paste

200 g (7 oz) shallots, peeled

10–15 dried chillies, seeds
  removed and soaked in
  hot water to rehydrate,
  then squeezed to remove
  excess water before using

2 large red chillies

1 clove garlic, peeled

5-cm (2-inch) knob ginger,
  peeled and sliced

3 stalks lemongrass, white
  part only, roughly chopped

250 ml (8 fl oz / 1 cup) water

Every family in Malaysia would have their own recipe for this dish. This is my family's version and we usually serve it during Eid. It's quite spicy, so it's not really the best thing to eat first thing in the morning, but it's a family tradition that we continue with.

....

- Wash the chicken and pat dry. Cut into 8 pieces. Set aside.

- Place the ingredients for the spice paste in a blender and process until smooth.

- Heat the oil in a wok over medium heat. Add the spice paste and fry for 30 minutes or until the oil separates. Add a little water every 15 minutes or whenever the mixture becomes too dry.

- Add the chicken, coconut milk, tamarind juice and salt. Bring to a boil, then turn down the heat and let it simmer for 20 minutes, or until the chicken is cooked through.

- Add the turmeric leaves and onion. Stir to mix and simmer for another 3 minutes.

- Dish out and serve hot with rice and other dishes.

AYAM GORENG, THE OLPINS
Olpin's Fried Chicken

Serves 6

1 large chicken, about 1.5 kg
(3 lb 4$^{1}/_{2}$ oz)

1 Tbsp turmeric powder

1 Tbsp chilli powder

1 tsp salt

3 Tbsp cornflour

1 egg, beaten

45 g (1$^{1}/_{2}$ oz) desiccated
coconut

2 stalks curry leaves, stems
discarded

Vegetable oil, as needed
for deep-frying

Spice Paste

3 shallots, peeled

2 cloves garlic, peeled

5-cm (2-inch) knob ginger,
peeled

Spice Powders

3 Tbsp coriander powder

2 tsp chilli powder

When it comes to fried chicken, I am sure every family has their own favourite recipe. Ours is Malaysian street food-inspired, spicy, fragrant, crispy and addictive. This is great on its own with a sweet chilli sauce or ketchup. I sometimes serve it with *nasi lemak* (page 20).

....

- Wash the chicken and pat dry. Cut into 8 pieces.

- Rub the chicken well with turmeric powder, chilli powder and salt. Set aside for 30 minutes.

- Pound the ingredients for the spice paste coarsely using a mortar and pestle. Set aside.

- Heat a dry pan and toast the spice powders until fragrant. Transfer to a bowl. Add the spice paste, cornflour, egg, desiccated coconut and curry leaves. Stir to combine.

- Coat the marinated chicken with this paste and set aside for at least 1 hour.

- Heat sufficient oil for deep-frying in a pan over medium heat. Gently lower the chicken into the hot oil and deep-fry until brown and crispy.

- Remove and drain well on paper towels. Serve with a sweet chilli sauce or ketchup.

KARI AYAM
Chicken Curry

Serves 6

1 small chicken, about 1 kg (2 lb 3 oz)

3 Tbsp vegetable oil

1 stalk curry leaves, stem discarded

3 medium potatoes, peeled and cut into quarters

250 ml (8 fl oz / 1 cup) coconut milk

1 tsp salt, or to taste

100 ml (3 1/2 fl oz) double cream (optional)

2 plum tomatoes, cut into quarters

A handful of chopped coriander leaves

Tempering Spices

3 cloves

5-cm (2-inch) length cinnamon stick

2 star anise

4 cardamom pods

Spice Paste

3 shallots, peeled

2 cloves garlic, peeled

7.5-cm (3-inch) knob ginger, peeled

2 candlenuts

Spice Powders

2 Tbsp chilli powder

3 Tbsp coriander powder

1 tsp turmeric powder

2 tsp cumin powder

125 ml (4 fl oz / 1/2 cup) water

My Malaysian chicken curry is a spicy yet creamy dish that goes well with rice or bread. In Malaysia, the spice mix can be readily purchased from the wet market, although my parents used to make their own. They would wash the raw spices, dry them under the sun, toast them, then bring them to the mill to have them ground into powder. Having lived abroad for the past 18 years, often in places where I could not purchase Malaysian curry powder, I started mixing my own, although not to the same extent as my parents. I simply mix spice powders together. It took me a few attempts to get the mix right, but I finally got the thumbs up from my mum. Try it!

- Wash the chicken and pat dry. Cut into small pieces. Set aside.

- Pound the ingredients for the spice paste coarsely using a mortar and pestle. Set aside.

- Combine the spice powders in a bowl and add the water gradually, mixing it into a paste. Set aside.

- Heat the oil in a saucepan over medium heat. Add the tempering spices and curry leaves. Cover with a lid and let the spices splutter.

- Add the spice paste and fry until fragrant and slightly dry.

- Add the spice powder paste and stir quickly, making sure the mixture does not burn. Turn the heat to low and fry the spices for another 10 minutes, adding a little water if the mixture dries up.

- Add the chicken and potatoes and stir gently, making sure the chicken and potatoes are well-coated with the spices. Leave to simmer for 5 minutes.

- Add the coconut milk and bring to a boil. Add the salt and turn the heat to low. Let it simmer for 20 minutes until the potatoes are tender and the chicken is cooked through.

- Taste and adjust the seasoning, if needed. If it is too spicy for your liking, stir in the double cream. Add the tomatoes and coriander leaves. Simmer for another 3 minutes before removing from the heat.

- Serve hot with rice or bread.

RENDANG DAGING MUDAH
Basic Beef Rendang

Serves 8

1 kg (2 lb 3 oz) beef

85 ml (2¹⁄₂ fl oz / ¹⁄₃ cup) vegetable oil

435 ml (14 fl oz / 1³⁄₄ cups) thick coconut milk

40 g (1¹⁄₃ oz) palm sugar, or to taste

1 tsp salt, or to taste

2 tsp turmeric powder

2 slices *asam gelugor*

100 g (3¹⁄₂ oz) toasted grated coconut (page 16)

8 kaffir lime leaves, thinly sliced

2 turmeric leaves, thinly sliced

Spice Paste

250 g (9 oz) shallots, peeled and coarsely chopped

4 cloves garlic, peeled and coarsely chopped

5-cm (2-inch) knob ginger, peeled and coarsely chopped

7.5-cm (3-inch) knob galangal, peeled and coarsely chopped

4 stalks lemon grass, ends trimmed

5-cm (2-inch) knob turmeric, peeled and coarsely chopped or 1 tsp turmeric powder

4 red chillies, or to taste

5 bird's eye chillies, or to taste

150 g (5¹⁄₃ oz) dried chilli paste (page 16)

200 ml (6³⁄₄ fl oz) thick coconut milk

Dry Spices

1 Tbsp coriander seeds

1 tsp cumin seeds

1 tsp fennel seeds

This is a quick version of rendang and I must emphasise that this dish is nothing like curry. The sauce is slightly dry, and the beef is chunky and flavourful, having absorbed all the flavour from the coconut milk and spices. Although it is an easy rendang, you will still have to go through the process of simmering the beef for several hours. To make a vegetarian version, substitute the beef with jackfruit.

··

- Cut the beef into even-sized chunks. Set aside.

- Place all the ingredients for the spice paste in a blender and process until smooth. Add a little water to help the blades move, if needed.

- Heat a dry pan and toast the dry spices until fragrant. Set aside to cool before pounding using a mortar and pestle.

- Heat the oil in a non-stick pan over medium heat. Add the spice paste and fry for 2 minutes. Add the pounded dry spices and fry for another 10 minutes.

- Add the beef, coconut milk, palm sugar, salt, turmeric powder and *asam gelugor*. Bring to a boil, then turn the heat down, and let it simmer, uncovered, for 1 hour or until the beef is tender. Check it every 15 minutes to make sure there is enough liquid in the rendang to keep it from burning. Add a little water, if needed.

- When the beef is cooked and tender, add the toasted grated coconut and cook for a further 10 minutes. The rendang is ready when the oil separates and the sauce is thick and creamy.

- Add the kaffir lime leaves and turmeric leaves. Dish out and serve with rice and other dishes.

NOTE Turmeric leaves can be omitted from the recipe if they are not available. This will not affect the taste of the rendang.

RENDANG OPOR PAHANG
Rendang from My Home Town

Serves 8

There is no right or wrong way to making this rendang. It is completely up to the individual, or in my case, my husband! Your rendang can have lots of gravy or be as dry as you like. In my home town of Pahang, this is usually served quite dry. It is popularly served at weddings and especially during Eid celebrations. This dish requires a lot of patience as it takes a good few hours to prepare. Don't be put off by the long list of ingredients. I have organised them to make it easy to follow.

1 kg (2 lb 3 oz) beef

85 ml (2½ fl oz / ⅓ cup) vegetable oil

750 ml (24 fl oz / 3 cups) coconut milk

2–3 Tbsp tamarind juice (page 17)

1 stalk lemongrass, white part only, bruised

4 Tbsp thick dark soy sauce

40 g (1⅓ oz) palm sugar

1 tsp salt, or to taste

3 Tbsp toasted grated coconut (page 16)

Opor Powder
20 dried chillies, seeds removed and cut into short lengths

2 Tbsp coriander seeds

½ tsp cumin seeds

2 tsp fennel seeds

6 cardamom pods, seeds removed

½ tsp nutmeg powder

4 cloves

2 tsp black peppercorns

Tempering Spices
2 star anise

2 cardamom pods

3 cloves

7.5-cm (3-inch) length cinnamon stick

Spice Paste
175 g (6 oz) shallots, peeled

1 medium white onion, peeled and cut into quarters

4 cloves garlic, peeled

1 tsp fermented prawn paste, toasted (optional)

5-cm (2-inch) knob ginger, peeled and sliced

3 stalks lemongrass, white part only, roughly chopped

5 Tbsp dried chilli paste (page 16)

250 ml (8 fl oz / 1 cup) water

- Wash, then cut the beef into cubes. Set aside.

- Prepare the *opor* powder. Heat a dry pan and toast the ingredients for the *opor* powder until fragrant. Set aside to cool, then grind to a fine powder using a spice grinder. We will use only half the mixture in this recipe. Store the remainder in an airtight container for use another time. It will keep for up to 3 months.

- Place the ingredients for the spice paste in a blender and process until fine. Set aside.

- Heat the oil in a large wok over medium heat. Add the tempering spices and fry until it starts to splutter. Add the spice paste and fry for 5 minutes until slightly dry and fragrant.

- Add the beef cubes and two-thirds of the coconut milk. Bring to a boil.

- Mix 4 Tbsp *opor* powder with the remaining coconut milk and add to the wok. Stir to mix, then bring to a boil. Turn down the heat and let it simmer for about 1 hour 30 minutes, or until the beef is tender.

- Add the tamarind juice, lemongrass, thick dark soy sauce, palm sugar, salt and toasted grated coconut. Let it simmer for another 15–30 minutes, until the oil separates and the gravy is thick. Taste and adjust the seasoning, if needed.

- Serve hot with rice and other dishes.

RENDANG TOK KAK UTEH
Grandma's Rendang

Serves 6

1 kg (2 lb 3 oz) beef, roast
   joint

2 slices *asam gelugor*

175 g (6 oz) dried chilli paste
   (page 16)

1 litre (32 fl oz / 4 cups)
   coconut milk

2 Tbsp chopped dark palm
   sugar, or to taste

1 tsp salt, or to taste

110 g (4 oz) toasted grated
   coconut (page 16)

2 turmeric leaves, finely
   sliced

Spice Powders

1 Tbsp coriander powder

2 tsp cumin powder

1 tsp black pepper powder

Whole Spices

2 cinnamon sticks

4 star anise

2 cloves

4 cardamom pods

Fresh Spices

325 g (11 oz) shallots, peeled
   and thinly sliced

4 cloves garlic, peeled and
   thinly sliced

7.5-cm (3-inch) knob
   galangal, peeled and thinly
   sliced

5-cm (2-inch) knob ginger,
   peeled and thinly sliced

5 stalks lemongrass, white
   part only, thinly sliced

I learnt to make this rendang from my late sister-in-law, who came from Perak. All the ingredients in this dish are chopped, nothing is blended, except for the dried chilli paste. The first time I saw her making this rendang, I was sceptical and wondered how the flavour of the spices would infuse the meat as everything is chopped. Needless to say, I was very impressed. The rendang was delicious, with the spices coating the meat, and the meat meltingly tender.

- Wash, then slice the beef thinly. Set aside.

- Heat a dry pan and toast the spice powders until fragrant. Rub this mixture all over the sliced beef. Cover and set aside for 4 hours.

- Place the beef in a large wok and add the whole spices and fresh spices, *asam gelugor*, dried chilli paste, coconut milk, palm sugar and salt. Bring to a boil, then turn the heat down and let it simmer for 1 hour. Stir it occasionally to make sure there is enough liquid and the mixture does not burn. After an hour, the beef should be tender and the sauce should have reduced considerably. Simmer for a further 30 minutes, if needed.

- Add the toasted grated coconut and turmeric leaves. Mix well and let it simmer for another 20 minutes. The gravy should be very thick and almost dry.

- Serve hot with rice and other dishes.

NOTE If *asam gelugor* is not available, replace with 2 Tbsp tamarind juice (page 17).

SUP KAMBING MAMAK
Spicy Mamak-style Lamb Soup

Serves 4

500 g (1 lb 1½ oz) lamb, shanks or shoulders, with some bone to give the soup a rich and robust flavour

Lemon juice, as needed

2 Tbsp vegetable oil

1.5 litres (48 fl oz / 6 cups) water

2 medium tomatoes, diced

2 medium potatoes, peeled and cut into bite-sized chunks

2 medium carrots, peeled and cut into bite-sized chunks

2 celery sticks (optional), diced

Salt, to taste

A handful of chopped coriander leaves

1 Tbsp crisp-fried shallots

Spice A

3 Tbsp coriander seeds

1½ tsp cumin seeds

1 tsp fennel seeds

1 tsp white peppercorns

1 tsp black peppercorns

Spice B

150 g (5⅓ oz) shallots, peeled

2 bird's eye chillies

3 cloves garlic, peeled

25 g (⅘ oz) ginger, peeled and grated

20 blanched almonds

2 candlenuts

250 ml (8 fl oz / 1 cup) water

Tempering Spices

3 cloves

3 cardamom pods

5-cm (2-inch) length cinnamon stick

2 star anise

The *mamak* are Indian-Muslim Malaysians who migrated to Malaysia from Kerala and Tamil Nadu in South India during the 19th century. This lamb soup is a popular *mamak* dish that Malaysians enjoy eating, and it is especially warming during the rainy season. It is best enjoyed with thick slices of white bread or baguette.

- Toast the ingredients for spice A in a dry pan over low heat until fragrant. Set aside to cool, then grind into a fine powder using a spice grinder. You can make a big batch of this spice and store it in an airtight container. It will last for months.

- Place the ingredients for spice B in a blender and process until fine. Set aside.

- Trim fat on lamb and cut into cubes. Wash with a little lemon juice to get rid of the fat and reduce any gamey smell.

- Heat the oil in a large heavy-bottom pan over medium heat. Add the tempering spices and fry until it starts to splutter. Add spice B and stir continuously over medium-low heat.

- Add a little water to spice A to make a thick paste. Add to the pan and keep stirring until it is almost dry. Turn up the heat to high and add the lamb cubes. Cook, stirring for about 3 minutes.

- Add the water and bring to a boil, then turn down the heat and let it simmer for at least 45 minutes. Keep an eye on the pot and add more water as needed.

- After 45 minutes, check that the lamb is tender and cooked through. Simmer for another 30 minutes, if needed.

- Add the vegetables and season to taste with salt. Simmer until the vegetables are tender.

- Serve hot, garnished with coriander leaves and crisp-fried shallots.

Vegetables, Salads and Pickles

ACAR TIMUN DAN LOBAK
Cucumber and Carrot Pickle

Serves 4

1 Tbsp ghee (clarified butter)

1 tsp mustard seeds

1 stalk curry leaves, stem discarded

2 Tbsp dried chilli paste (page 16)

1 carrot, peeled and cut into thin strips

1 green chilli, cut into thin strips

2 cucumbers, cored and cut into thin strips

1 medium white onion, peeled and cut into thin rounds

1 tsp roasted white sesame seeds (optional)

Spice Paste

1 clove garlic, peeled

2 shallots, peeled

5-cm (2-inch) ginger, peeled

Sauce

2 Tbsp ketchup

2 Tbsp sweet chilli sauce (page 138)

3 Tbsp white vinegar

3 Tbsp sugar

3 Tbsp honey

Salt, to taste

In Malaysia, pickled vegetables are known as *acar*. Besides vegetable *acar*, there is also a wide range of fruit *acar*. Each state and culture in Malaysia has their own versions of *acar* and every single one of them is delicious! *Acar* can be made ahead and stored in airtight jars for weeks. There are also some types of *acar* that can be made and consumed on the same day. This particular *acar* goes well with *nasi minyak* (page 24) and *kari ayam* (page 78).

- Pound the ingredients for the spice paste coarsely using a mortar and pestle. Set aside.

- Melt the ghee in a wok over medium heat. Add the mustard seeds and curry leaves. Cover with a lid and let the mustard seeds splutter.

- Add the spice paste and fry until fragrant and starting to brown. Add the dried chilli paste and cook for at least 10 minutes over low heat, until the oil separates. Add water, a little at a time, if the paste becomes too dry.

- Add the ingredients for the sauce and stir to mix. Let it simmer until the sauce is thick and sticky.

- Add the carrot and green chilli and cook for 2 minutes.

- Add the cucumbers and onion and turn the heat off, letting the cucumber and onion soften in the residual heat of the sauce.

- Taste and adjust the seasoning, if needed. The sauce should be sweet and sour with a hint of chilli.

- Transfer to a clean bowl and sprinkle with roasted sesame seeds, if desired. Serve as a side dish.

ACAR NENAS SAFFRON
Saffron and Pineapple Pickle

Serves 4

1 small pineapple, peeled and cored

1 medium white onion, peeled and sliced

4 cloves

2 Tbsp ghee (clarified butter)

1 tsp saffron

50 g (1³/₄ oz) sugar

Salt, to taste

A drop of yellow food colouring

This pickle has Arabic influence as it features saffron, which is not a common ingredient in Malaysian cooking. I learnt to make this from my late uncle who was a famous caterer in Singapore. This pickle goes well with *ayam masak merah* (page 74) and rice.

....

- Cut the pineapple into thick rounds, then into quarters. Place in a shallow pan.

- Add the other ingredients to the pan and cook over low heat for about 15 minutes, or until the pineapple is tender. Keep turning the pineapple pieces to make sure it cooks evenly.

- Transfer to a serving bowl and serve.

JELATAH MANGGA DENGAN LADA BENGGALA MASTERCHEF UK
My MasterChef UK Mango and Pepper Salad

Serves 4

1 medium red capsicum (bell pepper), cored and diced

1 medium green capsicum (bell pepper), cored and diced

1 small red onion, peeled and finely chopped

A handful of coriander leaves, finely chopped

1–2 Tbsp lime juice

1–2 Tbsp of sugar

1 tsp salt

1 large medium ripe mango, peeled and diced

This colourful salad is not only pretty, it is also very refreshing and moreish! I served this with fish cutlets on MasterChef UK, and I received fantastic reviews from all the judges. This simple and quick salad delivers a burst of flavour and also acts a palate cleanser. It will keep for a day or two in the fridge, so I always make extra to snack on.

....

- Place the capsicums, onion and coriander in a large bowl.

- Place the lime juice, sugar and salt in another bowl. Beat with a whisk, then add to the capsicum mixture. Toss to mix.

- Taste and adjust the seasoning, if needed. Gently stir in the diced mango just before serving.

KACANG PANJANG GORENG BERLADA
Stir-fried Spicy Long Beans

Serves 4

1 Tbsp vegetable oil

250 g (9 oz) long beans, ends trimmed and sliced on the diagonal into 5-cm (2-inch) lengths

2 kaffir lime leaves, thinly sliced

1 firm tofu square, diced and crisp-fried (optional)

Spice Paste

3 cloves garlic, peeled

2 shallots, peeled

1 large red chilli

2 bird's eye chillies

1 Tbsp dried anchovies, soaked in water for 5 minutes to soften

Long beans are also known as asparagus beans, yard long beans or Chinese long beans. In Malaysia, they are typically stir-fried or added to curries. This particular stir-fry is how I like to eat my long beans, always with a hint of chilli. Adjust the amount of chillies added to taste.

- Chop the ingredients for the spice paste roughly, then pound using a mortar and pestle into a coarse paste.

- Heat the oil in a wok over medium heat. Add the pounded spice paste and cook, stirring continuously, for 5–10 minutes, until the oil separates.

- Add the long beans and mix well. Leave to cook for about 3 minutes, until the beans are slightly soft.

- Turn the heat off and add the kaffir lime leaves and tofu. Stir to mix and dish out. Serve with rice and other dishes.

KOBIS GORENG DENGAN TELUR
Stir-fried Cabbage with Egg

Serves 4

1/4 tsp sesame oil

1 Tbsp vegetable oil

1 medium white onion, peeled and thinly sliced

3 cloves garlic, peeled and thinly sliced

1 red chilli, cut into fine strips

1 green chilli, cut into fine strips

1/2 tsp turmeric powder

200 g (7 oz) white cabbage, thinly sliced

1 egg, lightly beaten

A dash of light soy sauce

Salt, to taste

This stir-fry was my late dad's favourite dish. He loved anything with cabbage, whether cooked in a curry, stir-fried, or boiled and eaten with *sambal belacan*.

- Heat both the oils in a wok over a medium heat. Add the onion and garlic and stir-fry until soft. Add the red and green chillies, turmeric powder and cabbage. Turn up the heat and stir-fry for 2 minutes or until the cabbage is softened.

- Push the vegetables aside and add the egg. Quickly stir the egg into the vegetables and cook for 2–3 minutes until the vegetables are dry but still crisp.

- Season with light soy sauce and salt. Mix well. Dish out and serve hot with rice and other dishes.

KACANG BUNCIS GORENG DENGAN SOS TIRAM
Stir-fried French Beans with Oyster Sauce

Serves 4

1 Tbsp vegetable oil

2 cloves garlic, peeled and thinly sliced

1 medium white onion, peeled and thinly sliced

1 red chilli, cut into fine strips

150 g (5^1/$_3$ oz) French beans, ends trimmed and cut into 5-cm (2-inch) lengths

1 Tbsp oyster sauce

1 tsp light soy sauce

This is one of my favourite vegetable stir-fries! The savouriness of the oyster sauce goes really well with the French beans.

- Heat the oil in a wok over medium heat. Add the garlic and onion and stir-fry until the onion is translucent. Add the chilli and French beans and stir-fry for 3–4 minutes.

- Season with the oyster sauce and light soy sauce. Turn up the heat and stir-fry until the vegetables are tender.

- Dish out and serve hot with rice and other dishes.

SOLOK LADA
Stuffed Green Chillies

Serves 4–6

10 large green chillies

250 ml (8 fl oz / 1 cup) coconut milk

Stuffing

250 g (9 oz) basa, Spanish mackerel or cod fillet

100 g (3^1/$_2$ oz) freshly grated coconut

3 shallots, peeled and finely chopped

1 tsp fenugreek seeds

3 Tbsp sugar

1 tsp lime juice

1 tsp salt

Another popular dish from the East Coast of Malaysia that showcases fish. These stuffed chillies go well with rice and traditional Malay curries.

- Prepare the stuffing. Place the fish fillet in a pan and add just enough water to cover the fish. Poach for 10 minutes, then drain and set aside to cool.

- Pound the fish using a mortar and pestle and transfer to a mixing bowl. Add the remaining ingredients for the stuffing and mix well. Set aside.

- Rinse the chillies and pat dry. Slit the chillies lengthwise and remove the seeds.

- Fill the chillies with the fish stuffing and arrange, slit side up, on a baking dish that fits into your steamer.

- Pour the coconut milk over the chillies and steam for 20 minutes, or until the chillies are tender and most of the coconut milk has been absorbed.

- Serve immediately with rice and a curry.

Light Bites and Snacks

SATAY AYAM
Chicken Satay

Serves 4–6

300 g (11 oz) boneless
   chicken thighs, cut into
   small pieces

Bamboo skewers, soaked in
   water for a couple of hours
   before using

Marinade

3 stalks lemongrass, white
   part only, roughly chopped

85 g (3 oz) shallots, peeled

2 tsp coriander seeds,
   toasted

2 tsp fennel seeds, toasted

2 tsp cumin seeds, toasted

50–100 g (1¾–3½ oz)
   chopped palm sugar,
   added according to taste

3 tsp turmeric powder

Lemongrass Oil

1 stalk lemongrass

125 ml (4 fl oz / ½ cup)
   vegetable oil

An all-time favourite dish in Malaysia! Meat marinated in a variety of spices, then skewered and grilled to perfection, and served with peanut sauce. When I was a little girl, eating satay was considered a luxury and it was served only on special occasions. Some families continue this tradition and serve satay for Eid and birthdays, but satay is now widely available throughout Malaysia, from roadside stalls to high-end restaurants.

• Place all the ingredients for the marinade in a food processor and blend until fine without adding any water. Transfer the paste to a large bowl. Add the chicken pieces and mix well. Cover and refrigerate for at least 8 hours, or if time permits, overnight.

• Wipe the bamboo skewers dry. Thread 5–6 chicken pieces onto each skewer to fill about one-third of the skewer.

• Just before cooking, prepare the lemongrass oil to give the satay an extra flavour boost. Bruise the bulbous root end of the lemongrass and place root-side down in a small jug. Add the vegetable oil.

• To cook the satay, place the skewers on a barbecue or hot plate. Cook for 3 minutes on each side, basting with the lemongrass oil frequently.

• Serve the satay with peanut sauce (page 140) and wedges of cucumber and onions on the side.

NOTE Satay can also be made using beef, lamb, venison or veal. In Malaysia, satay is always served with compressed rice cakes known as *nasi himpit* or *ketupat nasi* (shown in the photo here). The rice is boiled in a bag until it is fully cooked and compressed. It is then cooled and cut into cubes.

KATLET IKAN MASTERCHEF UK
My MasterChef UK Fish Cutlets

Serves 4

150 g (5⅓ oz) basa fillets, or any white-flesh fish

160 g (5½ oz) potatoes

A pinch of salt

1 medium white onion, peeled and finely chopped

2 garlic cloves, peeled and finely chopped

4-cm (1½-inch) knob ginger, peeled and grated

2 stalks coriander leaves, finely chopped

1 stalk curry leaves, stem discarded, leaves finely chopped

1 green chilli, finely chopped

1 Tbsp curry powder

¼ tsp fennel seeds

1 egg yolk

A pinch of turmeric powder

White pepper powder, to taste

1–2 egg whites, lightly beaten

Vegetable oil, as needed for deep-frying

This dish is very special to me. My late mum taught me how to make these cutlets and I made them for my MasterChef UK challenge for which I received outstanding comments from the judges. These cutlets can be enjoyed as a snack with sweet chilli sauce or as an accompaniment to a main course.

- Place the fish in a small pot and add just enough water to cover the fish. Simmer over low heat until the fish is cooked through. Transfer the fish to a mixing bowl and set aside to cool.

- Peel the potatoes and chop roughly. Place in a small pot and add enough water to cover the potatoes. Add a pinch of salt and boil until the potatoes are softened. Drain and add to the bowl of fish.

- Add all the other ingredients, except for the egg whites and oil. Using a potato masher, mix all the ingredients until well combined.

- Form the mixture into small 5-cm (2-inch) patties.

- Heat sufficient oil for deep-frying in a frying pan over medium heat.

- Coat the patties in egg white, then gently lower into the hot oil and deep-fry until golden brown. Remove and set aside to drain.

- Enjoy with sweet chilli sauce or serve with a salad, such as my mango and pepper salad (page 92), on the side.

KERABU DAGING
Beef Salad

Serves 4

300 g (11 oz) beef, tenderloin or steak cut

1 Tbsp dried shrimps, toasted and coarsely pounded

Chopped roasted peanuts

Vegetables and Herbs

3 tomatoes, seeded and diced

5 bird's eye chillies, thinly sliced

2 stalks lemongrass, white part only, thinly sliced

2 red chillies, thinly sliced

1 medium red onion, peeled and thinly sliced

A handful of chopped coriander leaves

3 kaffir lime leaves, thinly sliced

Sauce

2 Tbsp toasted grated coconut (page 16)

3 Tbsp lime juice, or to taste

1 tsp minced garlic

A pinch of white pepper powder

Salt, to taste

Sugar, to taste

The Malay word *kerabu* can be loosely translated as salad. It is a dish where fruits, vegetables and, oftentimes, grilled meats, are mixed with lots of different herbs and spices. The tangy sauce is best drizzled over the dish at the last minute before eating. There are many variations of *kerabu*. It is a dish enjoyed by many as it can be eaten on its own, with rice or as a side dish. This is my version of *kerabu* and you are free to add other vegetables such as cucumber or bean sprouts to jazz it up.

....

- Bring a small pot of water to the boil. Add the beef and simmer over low heat until the beef is cooked through.

- Remove the beef and set aside to cool before cutting into very thin, almost see-through slices.

- Place the sliced beef into a large mixing bowl. Add the vegetables and herbs and dried shrimps. Set aside.

- Combine the ingredients for the sauce.

- Just before serving, toss everything together and check for seasoning. Garnish with chopped roasted peanuts and serve immediately.

TAUHU SUMBAT
Stuffed Tofu

Serves 4

6 firm tofu squares

500 ml (16 fl oz / 2 cups) vegetable oil

1 medium cucumber, core removed and finely shredded

1 carrot, peeled and finely shredded

1 cup bean sprouts, tailed

Sauce

1 red chilli

1 bird's eye chilli

2 shallots, peeled

1 clove garlic, peeled

125 ml (4 fl oz / ½ cup) tamarind juice (page 17)

60 g (2 oz) sugar

½ tsp salt

80 g (2⅘ oz) roasted peanuts, roughly chopped

This vegan dish is popularly eaten as a snack in Malaysia. It is sold at roadside stalls and is especially popular during Ramadan. This dish is especially dear to me as it brings back fond memories of my days in secondary school. We were taught to prepare this during a Home Economics class and I thought frying tofu would be a piece of cake. Alas, I made a mess of it!

- Cut each square of tofu diagonally to get two triangles. Pat dry with paper towels to ensure it doesn't splatter when frying.

- Heat the oil and gently lower the tofu into the hot oil. Deep-fry until golden brown and crispy on the outside. Remove and set aside to cool.

- Cut a slit in the middle of each triangle of tofu and stuff with cucumber, carrot and bean sprouts. Cover and set aside.

- To prepare the sauce, place the chillies, shallots and garlic in a blender and process until fine. Heat 2 tsp oil in a saucepan and fry the paste until fragrant. Add the tamarind juice, sugar and salt. Mix well and let it simmer until thickened to a pourable consistency. Add the peanuts and transfer to a serving bowl.

- Spoon some sauce into the tofu pockets and enjoy. It will be messy, but it is well worth the mess!

POPIAH SAYUR
Vegetable Spring Rolls

Serves 4

1 packet frozen spring rolls skins

1 Tbsp plain flour

Vegetable oil, as needed for deep-frying

Filling

2 tsp vegetable oil

1/2 tsp sesame oil

2 cloves garlic, peeled and minced

1 firm tofu square, mashed

75 g (2²/₃ oz) carrot, peeled and shredded

50 g (1³/₄ oz) green cabbage, shredded

50 g (1³/₄ oz) French beans, thinly sliced

50 g (1³/₄ oz) yam bean or turnip, peeled and shredded

25 g (⁴/₅ oz) spring onions, thinly sliced

A pinch of salt

1/2 tsp white pepper powder

1 tsp sweet soy sauce

Spring rolls are a popular snack throughout Asia. There are many versions even within Malaysia and every household will also have their personal take on the filling. Mine is a simple vegetarian version that I learnt to make from my Chinese neighbour while growing up. These are best served hot, with a dip of sweet chilli sauce.

....

- Remove the packet of frozen spring roll skins from the freezer and leave on the countertop to thaw for at least 30 minutes.

- Prepare the filling. Heat both the oils in a non-stick wok over medium heat. Add the garlic and fry until fragrant.

- Add the mashed tofu and fry gently for 1 minute. Turn the heat up and add all the vegetables. Mix well and season with salt, pepper and sweet soy sauce. Cook for another minute, then transfer to a bowl and set aside to cool.

- Mix the flour with a little water to get a thick paste. Set aside.

- Place a spring roll skin on your worktop. Place a spoonful of the filling along the edge nearest to you. Fold the right and left edges of the skin over to cover the filling, then start rolling into a log. Brush the remaining edge of the spring roll skin with some flour paste and seal. Set aside. Repeat with the remaining ingredients.

- Heat sufficient oil for deep-frying in a wok over medium heat. Gently lower the spring rolls into the hot oil and fry until golden brown. Do this in small batches. Remove and drain well on paper towels.

- Serve with sweet chilli sauce (page 138).

KARIPAP PUSING
Spiral Curry Puffs

Makes 25–30 pieces

350 g (12 oz) potatoes, peeled and diced

Salt, as needed

Vegetable oil, as needed

3 cloves

2 cardamom pods

2 stalks curry leaves, stems discarded

2.5-cm (1-inch) length cinnamon stick

1 star anise

4 tsp minced garlic

1 Tbsp minced ginger

2 medium white onions, peeled and finely chopped

1 Tbsp curry powder

2 tsp chilli powder (optional)

150 g (5^1/$_3$ oz) minced chicken

1 Tbsp sugar, or to taste

125–250 ml (4–8 fl oz / ^{1}/$_2$–1 cup) water

A handful of finely chopped coriander leaves

Dough A

175 g (6 oz) plain flour

75 g (2^2/$_3$ oz) vegetable shortening

Dough B

185 g (6^1/$_2$ oz) plain flour

1 Tbsp sugar

^{1}/$_2$ tsp salt

35 g (1^1/$_4$ oz) cold unsalted butter, cut into small cubes

90–125 ml (3–4 fl oz / ^{3}/$_8$–^{1}/$_2$ cup) water

Almost every South East Asian country has a version of this scrumptious snack. Whenever I feel like it, I would whip up a big batch of these spiral curry puffs and freeze them. They can then be thawed and deep-fried for a quick snack. The key to these curry puffs is the thin, crispy and flaky crust.

....

- Prepare dough A. Combine the flour with the shortening to get a soft dough. Wrap with cling film and set aside.

- Prepare dough B. Mix the flour with the sugar and salt, then rub in the butter until the mixture resembles breadcrumbs. Add the water a little at a time, kneading to get a soft, smooth dough. You might not need to use all the water. Wrap with cling film and set aside.

- Prepare the filling. Boil a pot of water and add 1 tsp salt. Add the diced potatoes and boil until tender. Drain well and set aside.

- Heat 2 Tbsp oil in a pan over medium heat. Add the cloves, cardamom pods, curry leaves, cinnamon and star anise, and fry until fragrant. Turn the heat to low and add in the garlic and ginger. Stir to mix, then add the onions, curry powder and chilli powder, if desired. Leave it to cook for 2 minutes.

- Add the chicken and stir for about 10 minutes. Season with sugar and 1 tsp salt. Add the potatoes and water. Cook, stirring continuously over low heat for 5–10 minutes, until the mixture is soft and mushy, but not runny. Test by running your spatula across the base of the pan. It should take some time for the mixture to flow back.

- Add the coriander and mix well. Adjust the seasoning to taste. Turn off the heat and allow the filling to cool completely before using.

- Flatten dough B and wrap it around dough A. Roll the combined dough into a thin 40-cm (16-inch) square sheet, then roll up like a Swiss roll. Pinch the open edge to seal it.

- Cut the log into 25–30 discs, each about 1.5-cm (³/₄-inch) thick. You should be able to see a spiral pattern. This is known in Malay as *pusing*. Roll each disc into a 7.5-cm (3-inch) round. Spoon some filling onto each round and fold to enclose the filling. Pinch the edges, then crimp to seal. At this point, the curry puffs can be placed in a freezer bag and stored in the freezer for up to 2 months. Thaw before deep-frying.

- Heat sufficient oil for deep-frying in a wok over medium heat. Lower the curry puffs into the hot oil and deep-fry for 2 minutes on each side until golden brown and crisp. Do this in batches. Drain well and serve.

TEMBOSA
Fish and Coconut Curry Puffs

Makes 25–30 pieces

Vegetable oil, as needed
 for deep-frying

Dough
300 g (11 oz) plain flour
100 ml (3½ fl oz) vegetable oil
½ tsp salt
250 ml (8 fl oz / 1 cup) water

Filling
125 ml (4 fl oz / ½ cup) water
200 g (7 oz) Spanish mackerel
 fillet
1 tsp salt
90 g (3¼ oz) desiccated
 coconut
250 ml (8 fl oz / 1 cup)
 coconut cream
4 shallots, peeled and finely
 sliced
2 Tbsp slivered ginger
1 Tbsp sugar
1 tsp fenugreek seeds
2 tsp crushed black
 peppercorns

An East Coast version of curry puffs (page 110). Instead of chicken and potatoes, *tembosa* are filled with fish and grated coconut. It is an easy to-go snack that we all love — the only problem is that you can't stop eating them once you start! My fondest childhood memory of this snack are family picnics by the waterfall. So yes, these are perfect for packing into picnic baskets as well!

....

- Prepare the dough. Place the flour in a heatproof mixing bowl and set aside. Heat the vegetable oil with the salt in a small pot and bring it to its boiling point. Pour the hot oil into the flour. The flour will sizzle a little. Add the water and stir with a wooden spoon. Let the dough cool slightly, then knead until it is soft and smooth. Cover with cling film and set aside.

- Prepare the filling. Place the water in a small pan and bring to a boil. Add the fish and salt and let the fish cook.

- Remove the cooked fish and mash with a fork. Return the mashed fish to the pan and add the remaining ingredients. Stir continuously over low heat until the mixture is slightly dry. Taste and adjust the seasoning, if needed. Set aside to cool.

- Divide the dough in half and keep one portion wrapped in cling film to prevent it from drying out.

- Dust a clean work surface with some flour. Pinch off 20-g (⅔-oz) dough and roll into a ball. Flatten the dough into a disc and top with a spoonful of the filling. Fold the disc to enclose the filling, then pinch the edges and crimp to seal. Alternatively, create a pattern by pressing the edges with a fork. Repeat with the remaining ingredients.

- Heat sufficient oil for deep-frying in a wok over medium heat. Lower the curry puffs into the hot oil and deep-fry for 2 minutes on each side until golden brown and crisp. Do this in batches. Drain well and serve.

NOTE Another method to prepare the dough is to combine the oil, salt and water in a pot and bring it to a boil before mixing with the flour.

KEROPOK LEKOR
Malaysian Fish Sausage

Serves 8

250 g (9 oz) fish fillet
  (use Spanish mackerel,
  if available)

1 Tbsp sugar

1–2 tsp salt

1 tsp anchovy stock powder
  or fish stock powder
  (optional)

2 Tbsp + 1 tsp ice-cold water

85 g (3 oz) sago or tapioca
  flour + more as needed

Vegetable oil, as needed

This tasty deep-fried snack hails from Terengganu in Malaysia, but it is so popular, it can be found throughout Malaysia, from fancy restaurants to roadside stalls. It's not difficult to make, so try it!

- Place the fish fillet in a food processor and blend into a smooth paste. Add the sugar, salt, stock powder and ice-cold water and continue to blend for 1 minute until everything is incorporated.

- Transfer the mixture to a large bowl. Add the sago/tapioca flour while stirring until it forms a soft and pliable dough. Knead the mixture for about 3 minutes.

- Dust your hands and a work surface with some sago/tapioca flour. Pinch a spoonful of the fish mixture and form it into a sausage, about 4 cm (1½ inch) in diameter and 15 cm (6 inch) in length. Repeat with the remaining ingredients.

- Boil a large pot of water and lower the sausages in to cook. The sausages are done when they float.

- Transfer the cooked sausages to a colander and rub with vegetable oil to prevent them from sticking to each other. Set aside to cool.

- Enjoy the sausages as is or deep-fry until golden brown and crispy. Serve with *keropok* chilli sauce (page 138) on the side.

OTAK-OTAK
Grilled Fish Cakes in Banana Leaf

Makes 10 parcels

300 g (11 oz) fish fillet (use Spanish mackerel, if available)

Banana leaves, as needed

3 Tbsp vegetable oil

4 kaffir lime leaves, finely sliced

4 tsp lime juice

1 tsp salt

2 Tbsp sugar

1 egg, beaten

1 Tbsp cornflour

6 Tbsp coconut milk

45 g (1½ oz) desiccated coconut

Spice Paste

1 Tbsp dried chilli paste (page 16)

3 shallots, peeled

1 clove garlic, peeled

1 stalk lemongrass, white part only, roughly chopped

1 candlenut (optional)

1-cm (½-inch) knob galangal, peeled

The literal translation of the name of this dish is brain-brain. Apparently, it was so-named because of its resemblance to brains! This spicy, fragrant snack is a common street food in Malaysia. This is my family's recipe which has been modified to suit our preferences.

....

- Cut the fish into 10 pieces, each about 8 x 3-cm (3 x 1-inch). Set aside. Cut the banana leaves to get 10 rectangles, each about 25 x 15-cm (10 x 6-inch). Soak in boiling water for 3 minutes. This will soften them and make them pliable. Wipe dry and set aside.

- Place the ingredients for the spice paste in a blender and process until fine. Heat the oil in a deep pan over medium heat. Add the spice paste and fry until the oil separates. Add the kaffir lime leaves, lime juice, salt, sugar, egg, cornflour, coconut milk and desiccated coconut and mix well. Transfer to a bowl.

- Preheat the oven to 180°C (350°F).

- Place 1 tsp spice mixture on a banana leaf. Top with a piece of fish and cover with another 1 tsp spice mixture. Fold the long sides of the leaf over to enclose the filling, then fold the open ends under to create a neat parcel. Repeat with the remaining ingredients.

- Place the parcels on a baking tray and bake for 15 minutes. Serve warm.

NOTE These parcels can also be cooked in a steamer for 15 minutes. If banana leaves are not available, use aluminium foil.

CUCUR UDANG
Prawn Fritters

Serves 4

350 g (12 oz) plain flour

2 Tbsp cornflour

2 tsp baking powder

1 tsp turmeric powder

1 tsp salt

150 g (5$^1/_3$ oz) prawns, peeled and deveined

1 medium white onion, peeled and diced

3 spring onions, finely chopped

100 g (3$^1/_2$ oz) bean sprouts, tailed

85 g (3 oz) carrot, peeled and shredded

1 green chilli, finely chopped

250 ml (8 fl oz / 1 cup) water

Vegetable oil, as needed for deep-frying

Warning: These fritters are seriously addictive! Once cooked, they are crispy on the outside, and soft and fluffy on the inside. They make great party food as they can be prepared ahead, then kept warm in the oven.

....

• Place the plain flour, cornflour, baking powder, turmeric powder and salt in a mixing bowl. Mix well.

• Add the prawns, onion, spring onions, bean sprouts, carrot and chilli. Mix well so the flour mixture coats the prawns and vegetables.

• Add the water a little at a time, stirring until the batter is slightly loose but not runny. Set aside for 15 minutes for the baking powder to work.

• Heat sufficient oil for deep-frying in a wok over medium heat.

• Dip a small round metal ladle in the hot oil for few seconds to heat it up, then pour 1–2 Tbsp batter into the ladle. Lower the ladle quickly back into the hot oil to let the batter cook. As the batter cooks, it will loosen from the ladle. Turn the fritter over occasionally until it is evenly golden brown. Remove and drain well on paper towels.

• Repeat with the remaining ingredients.

• Serve warm with sweet chilli sauce (page 138) on the side.

NOTE Instead of using a ladle, you can also spoon the mixture directly into the hot oil and make uneven-sized fritters.

PULUT SAMBAL
Sticky Rice Bon Bon

Serves 6

375 g (13 oz) glutinous rice

250 ml (8 fl oz / 1 cup) coconut milk

375 ml (12 fl oz / 1¹/₂ cups) water

2 tsp vegetable oil

¹/₄ tsp salt

2 pandan leaves, rinsed and tied into a knot

Coconut Floss

1 Tbsp coriander seeds

¹/₂ tsp fennel seeds

¹/₂ tsp cumin seeds

¹/₄ tsp black pepper powder

2 Tbsp vegetable oil

175 g (6 oz) desiccated coconut

¹/₂ tsp salt

1 Tbsp sugar, or to taste

Spice Paste for Coconut Floss

2 stalks lemongrass, white part only, roughly chopped

2 cloves garlic, peeled

150 g (5¹/₃ oz) shallots, peeled

1-cm (¹/₂-inch) knob galangal, peeled

2 red chillies

125 ml (4 fl oz / ¹/₂ cup) coconut milk

This is a vegetarian version of a traditional savoury tea time snack. The creamy sticky rice complements the spicy and sweet tones of the coconut floss. This dish is also suitable for vegans.

- Soak the rice in water for 2 hours.

- Drain the rice, then place in a rice cooker with the coconut milk, water, oil and salt. Stir to mix. Add the pandan leaves and turn the rice cooker on to cook. When the rice is done, fluff the rice using a fork and set it aside to cool.

- Place the ingredients for the spice paste in a blender and process until smooth. Remove and set aside.

- Prepare the coconut floss. Heat a dry pan over medium heat. Add the coriander seeds, fennel seeds, cumin seeds and black pepper and toast until fragrant. Remove and set aside.

- Heat the oil in a pan over medium heat. Add the spice paste and fry until it is slightly dry and the oil separates.

- Add the desiccated coconut, toasted spices, salt and sugar. Turn the heat down and keep stirring until the coconut is dry. Transfer to a bowl and set it aside to cool.

- Take a tablespoonful of rice and roll it into a ball. Toss it in the coconut floss and coat well. Serve.

LEMPENG KELAPA
Coconut Pancakes

Serves 4

125 g (4½ oz) plain flour

45 g (1½ oz) desiccated coconut

2 shallots, peeled and thinly sliced

½ tsp salt

2 Tbsp melted butter + more as needed for cooking pancakes

250 ml (8 fl oz / 1 cup) water

Nothing beats dipping this traditional coconut pancake in sambal and enjoying it with a cup of strong coffee for breakfast. Delish! In Malaysia, freshly grated young coconut is used to give the pancake a rich, creamy flavour. As fresh grated coconut is not readily available in the UK, I use desiccated coconut.

- Combine the flour, desiccated coconut, shallots, salt and 2 Tbsp melted butter in a mixing bowl. Add the water and stir to get a very thick and almost lumpy batter. Set aside for 10 minutes.

- Heat a little butter in a non-stick frying pan over low heat. Pour a ladleful of the batter into the middle of the pan, then use the back of a wet spatula to push and flatten the batter into a 1-cm (½-inch) thick pancake. Let it cook for about 2 minutes.

- Top the pancake with 1 tsp butter and spread it out. Flip the pancake over and let it cook for another 2 minutes, or longer for a slightly darker and crispier pancake. Transfer to a plate and repeat with the remaining ingredients.

- Serve hot with *ayam masak merah* (page 74) or *kari ayam* (page 78).

Sweet
Treats

KEK PISANG KAMPUNG
Kampung-style Banana Cake

Makes one 20-cm (8-inch) round cake

185 g (6 1/2 oz) plain flour

1 tsp baking powder

1 tsp baking soda

3 medium, very ripe bananas

175 g (6 oz) sugar

85 ml (2 1/2 fl oz / 1/3 cup)
    vegetable oil

A pinch of salt

1 large egg at room
    temperature, lightly beaten

Icing sugar (optional)

This recipe has been in my family for as long as I can remember. My late mum used to bake it using an old-fashioned round oven and my siblings and I would sit by the oven to watch the cake bake through the oven's little round glass window. We often got burned when we got too close to the oven and that would result in us getting kicked out of the kitchen. The most agonising bit was smelling the freshly baked cake, but not being able to eat it as we always had to wait for my dad to come home from work!

- Preheat the oven to 180°C (350°F).

- Lightly grease a 20-cm (8-inch) round cake tin with butter and line with baking paper. Alternatively, grease the cake tin with butter and sprinkle with some flour. Shake the tin and discard any excess flour.

- Sift the flour, baking powder and baking soda into a bowl and set aside.

- Peel the bananas and place in a bowl. Mash, then add the sugar, oil, salt and egg. Stir to combine.

- Add the flour mixture and fold until just combined.

- Pour the mixture into the prepared cake tin. Place in the oven and bake for 35–40 minutes, or until the top of the cake springs back when lightly pressed.

- Remove the cake from the oven and place on a wire rack to cool for 15 minutes before unmoulding.

- Dust the cake with icing sugar, if desired, and serve.

KUIH BOM
Deep-fried Glutinous Rice Flour Balls with Sweet Coconut Filling

Makes 18–20 pieces

100 g (3 1/2 oz) white sesame
  seeds

Vegetable oil, as needed
  for deep-frying

Dough

240 g (8 1/2 oz) glutinous
  rice flour

60 g (2 1/2 oz) plain flour

1/2 tsp salt

250 ml (8 fl oz / 1 cup) water

Filling

100 g (3 1/2 oz) palm sugar,
  chopped

1 pandan leaf, rinsed
  and tied into a knot

85 ml (2 1/2 fl oz / 1/3 cup)
  water

500 g (1 lb 1 1/2 oz) desiccated
  coconut

These moreish, chewy snacks are known as *kuih bom* or *kuih bidaran*. These beauties sometimes explode while frying, hence the name! To avoid your *kuih bom* exploding while cooking, use very low heat. There are many variations of this snack — some recipes use only glutinous rice flour, some use a mixture of glutinous rice flour and sweet potatoes, and some use a mixture of rice flour and plain flour. Despite the differences, the aim is always to achieve a dough that will yield a crisp, chewy texture when deep-fried. Enjoy with a cup of black coffee.

....

- Prepare the filling. Place the palm sugar, pandan leaf and water in a wok and bring to a boil, stirring to dissolve the palm sugar.

- Add the desiccated coconut and cook over low heat, stirring continuously for 10 minutes, or until the coconut has absorbed all the liquid. Transfer to a bowl and set aside to cool.

- Prepare the dough. Place both the flours and salt in a bowl. Mix well, then add the water a little at a time while kneading to achieve a soft and smooth dough.

- Pinch off 25 g (4/5 oz) dough and roll into a ball. Flatten the dough into a disc and top with a spoonful of the filling. Bring the edges up to enclose the filling, then pinch to seal. Roll into a smooth ball. Coat with sesame seeds. Repeat with the remaining ingredients.

- Cover and place in the freezer for at least 1 hour before frying.

- Heat sufficient oil for deep-frying in a deep wok over medium heat. Turn down the heat until it is very low, then gently lower the balls into the hot oil and deep-fry until golden brown. Do this in batches. Drain well on paper towels.

- Set aside to cool before serving.

  **SweetTreats**

KUIH KETAYAP
Pandan Crepes with Sweet Coconut Filling

Serves 6–8

Vegetable oil, as needed

Batter
150 g (5$\frac{1}{3}$ oz) plain flour
$\frac{1}{4}$ tsp salt
1 egg, lightly beaten
250 ml (8 fl oz / 1 cup)
    pandan water (page 17)
4 Tbsp milk
2 Tbsp vegetable oil

Filling
100 g (3$\frac{1}{2}$ oz) palm sugar,
    chopped
1 pandan leaf, rinsed and
    tied into a knot
4 Tbsp water
270 g (9$\frac{1}{2}$ oz) desiccated
    coconut
1 tsp cornflour

This is one of the easiest and most delicious desserts to make. It goes by different names in different parts of Malaysia, so you might also know it as *dadar gulung, kuih gulung* or *kuih dadar*. It is essentially a crepe filled with sweetened grated coconut.

• Prepare the batter. Place all the ingredients for the batter into a blender and process for about 3 minutes until smooth. Strain the batter into a bowl and set aside.

• Prepare the filling. Place the palm sugar, pandan leaf and water into a small pot and bring to a boil. When the palm sugar is completely dissolved, add the desiccated coconut and stir continuously over low heat for 10 minutes. Add the cornflour and stir until there is no liquid left and the mixture is sticky. Set aside to cool.

• Heat a non-stick frying pan and lightly grease with oil. Pour a ladleful of the batter into the centre of the pan and swirl to make a thin crepe. Leave to cook for 1 minute, then flip the crepe over to cook for another minute on the other side. Transfer to a clean plate. Repeat with the remaining batter.

• To assemble, place a spoonful of the filling along the edge of the crepe nearest to you. Fold the edge over to enclose the filling, then fold the left and right edges over and start rolling into a log. Set aside.

• Repeat with the remaining ingredients. Serve.

ONDE-ONDE
Glutinous Rice Flour Balls with Palm Sugar Filling

Serves 4

200 g (7 oz) glutinous rice flour

150–200 ml (5–6¹/₃ fl oz) pandan water (page 17)

250 g (9 oz) freshly grated coconut

A pinch of salt

200 g (7 oz) palm sugar, chopped

These chewy glutinous rice flour balls are filled with cubes of palm sugar, then boiled and tossed in fragrant grated coconut. The boiling melts the palm sugar and when you take a bite, the sweet liquid will literally burst out, so be very careful!

- Place the glutinous rice flour in a bowl. Add the pandan water gradually, kneading to form a soft dough. Adjust by adding more pandan water or glutinous rice flour as necessary.

- Mix the grated coconut with the salt. Place in a bowl and set aside.

- Pinch a small tablespoonful of dough and flatten lightly. Place a few pieces of chopped palm sugar in the centre, then bring the edges up to enclose the palm sugar. Roll the dough into a smooth ball. Repeat with the remaining ingredients.

- Boil a pot of water and place the balls in to cook. Do this in batches. The balls are done when they float. Remove with a slotted spoon and gently shake off any excess water.

- Place the balls in the grated coconut and toss to coat. Enjoy!

SAGU GULA MELAKA
Sago with Palm Sugar and Coconut Cream

Serves 6

3 litres (96 fl oz / 12 cups) water

175 g (6 oz) sago pearls

Coconut Cream

400 ml (13 1/3 fl oz) coconut milk

A pinch of salt

Syrup

70 g (2 1/2 oz) palm sugar

6 Tbsp water

2–3 pandan leaves, rinsed and tied into a knot

This my cheeky monkey's favourite dessert. My Sofea would eat this every day if she could. It's a perfect dessert for a hot summer's day since everything is chilled before serving!

....

- Bring the water to the boil in a large pot and place the sago in to cook. Stir for 3 minutes, then turn the heat off and cover the pot with a lid. Set aside for 15 minutes, or until the sago is translucent.

- Pour the sago into a colander and rinse under running tap water for about a minute. Spoon the sago into individual moulds or bowls and refrigerate for at least an hour until chilled and firm.

- Prepare the coconut cream. Heat the coconut milk until it is warm, then add a pinch of salt. Set aside to cool before refrigerating to chill.

- Prepare the syrup. Place the palm sugar, water and pandan leaves in a small pot and bring to a boil. Turn down the heat and let it simmer until it is very thick. Set aside to cool before refrigerating to chill.

- Transfer the set sago puddings to serving bowls. Pour some syrup into each bowl, then drizzle with coconut cream. Serve cold.

Sweet
Chilli
Sauce

Keropok
Sauce

Sweet
Soy
Sauce

Nasi
Lemak
Sambal

Peanut
Sauce

Sauces
and
Condiments

Tomato
Sambal

KEROPOK CHILLI SAUCE
Sos Keropok

Makes about 500 g (1 lb 1¹/₂ oz)

225 g (8 oz) sugar

500 ml (16 fl oz / 2 cups) water

1 clove garlic, peeled

110 g (4 oz) dried chilli paste, or to taste (page 16)

250 ml (8 fl oz / 1 cup) white vinegar

2 tsp salt

In Malaysian homes, there is always a bottle of chilli sauce handy for enjoying with snacks or meals! This homemade chilli sauce goes well with almost anything! Try it with the *keropok lekor* (page 114).

- Place all the ingredients in a saucepan and bring to a boil. Turn the heat to low and let it simmer for 30 minutes to an hour, or until the sauce is thick and sticky.

- Discard the garlic and set aside to cool. Store in a clean glass jar. The sauce will keep for months in the refrigerator.

SWEET CHILLI SAUCE
Sos Cili Manis

Makes about 200 g (7 oz)

5–6 Tbsp white vinegar

100 g (3¹/₂ oz) sugar

4 Tbsp water

3 cloves garlic, peeled and minced

2 Tbsp chilli flakes

¹/₂ tsp salt, or to taste

1 tsp cornflour, mixed with 3 Tbsp water

This is the sweet chilli sauce that I served with my fish cutlets on MasterChef UK. The judges loved the balance of flavours in this sauce! Double the recipe to make a bigger batch as this will go fast!

- Place all the ingredients, except the cornflour paste, into a heavy-bottom pan and bring to a boil. Turn down the heat and let it simmer for 15 minutes.

- Stir in the cornflour paste and let it simmer for another 2 minutes. Remove from the heat and set aside to cool. The chilli sauce will thicken as it cools.

- Store in a clean glass jar. The sauce will keep for up to a month in the refrigerator.

SWEET SOY SAUCE DIP
Sambal Kicap

Serves 6

2 red chillies

3 bird's eye chillies

1 shallot, peeled and diced

4 Tbsp sweet soy sauce

1 Tbsp lime or lemon juice

Salt, to taste

This dip goes well with *ayam goreng* (page 76) and white rice. It is also delicious with *mee hoon sup berempah* (page 38). For a less spicy sauce, use just one bird's eye chilli.

• Remove the seeds from the red chillies for a less spicy sauce. Chop the red chillies and bird's eye chillies finely. Place in a small bowl.

• Add the shallot, sweet soy sauce, lime/lemon juice and salt and mix well. Serve in small saucers.

TOMATO SAMBAL
Sambal Tomato

Serves 6

2 Tbsp vegetable oil

3 shallots, peeled and thinly sliced

2.5-cm (1-inch) fermented prawn paste, toasted

4 medium tomatoes, diced

2 large red chillies, seeds removed and finely chopped

2 red bird's eye chillies, seeds removed and finely chopped

1 Tbsp sugar

1 tsp salt

4 Tbsp tamarind juice (page 17)

I was introduced to this sambal by a friend from Singapore. She would make it whenever we had lunch together at her place. Her sambal is much spicier, with a more pungent taste of fermented prawn paste. Personally, I prefer it to be milder, especially in terms of the fermented prawn paste, so I've tweaked it in this recipe.

• Heat 2 Tbsp oil in a wok over medium heat and fry the shallots and fermented prawn paste until combined.

• Add the tomatoes and fry for 30 seconds. Add the rest of the ingredients and let it simmer for 10 minutes. Taste and adjust the seasoning, if needed.

• Set aside to cool. Store in a clean glass jar. The sauce will keep for months in the refrigerator.

PEANUT SAUCE
Kuah Kacang

Makes about 3 litres (96 fl oz / 12 cups)

500 g (1 lb 1^1/$_2$ oz) peanuts,
  roasted

Water, as needed

6 Tbsp vegetable oil

100 g (3^1/$_2$ oz) palm sugar

1 tsp salt

1 Tbsp tamarind juice
  (page 17)

Spice Paste

150 g (5^1/$_2$ oz) shallots,
  peeled

85 g (3 oz) dried chilli paste,
  or to taste (page 16)

4 stalks lemongrass, white
  part only, roughly chopped

250 ml (8 fl oz / 1 cup) water

This sauce is traditionally served with satay (page 100). However, in our household, we eat it with everything! It is especially delicious with fried rice or as a base for pizza! Strange, I know!

....

- Place half the peanuts in the blender with 250 ml (8 fl oz / 1 cup) water and process into a coarse paste. Transfer to a large bowl and set aside.

- Repeat to blend the remaining peanuts with another 250 ml (8 fl oz / 1 cup) water, but process until fine. Transfer to the bowl and mix well.

- Place the ingredients for the spice paste in the blender and process until fine. Set aside.

- Heat the oil in a heavy-bottom pot over medium heat. Add the spice paste and fry for about 15 minutes. Add the blended peanuts and 250 ml (8 fl oz / 1 cup) water to the pot and stir. This will make the sauce slightly runny.

- Turn down the heat and continue cooking the peanut sauce until the oil separates. This will take 45 minutes to an hour.

- Add the palm sugar, salt and tamarind juice. Mix well, then taste and adjust the seasoning, if needed. Let it simmer for another 10 minutes before removing from the heat.

- Serve the sauce with satay and sides of cucumber and onions.

NOTE This sauce can be enjoyed with salads, boiled potatoes, chips, cheese, fried rice, and almost anything, really! Cook a big batch and freeze in small portions, then thaw when needed. It will keep for months. To thaw, simply leave on the countertop for a few hours, then place over very low heat.

NASI LEMAK SAMBAL
Sambal Nasi Lemak Bawang

Serves 10

125 ml (4 fl oz / ½ cup)
  vegetable oil

2 slices *asam gelugor* or
  2 tsp tamarind juice
  (page 17)

½ tsp salt

Dark brown sugar, to taste

1 medium white onion,
  peeled and sliced

Spice Paste

20 dried chillies, seeds
  removed and soaked in
  hot water to rehydrate,
  then squeezed to remove
  excess water before using

4 red chillies, roughly
  chopped

300 g (11 oz) shallots, peeled
  and roughly chopped

2 large white onions, peeled
  and roughly chopped

2 cloves garlic, peeled

4 stalks lemongrass, white
  part only, roughly chopped

In South East Asia, sambal is the standard name for any spicy dish where blended chillies are the main ingredient. This is a basic vegetarian sambal that I always make to accompany my *nasi lemak* (page 20), purely because my family is not too keen on other sambals. I have included a note on how to make anchovy sambal below.

....

- Place all the ingredients for the spice paste in a blender and process until smooth. Set aside.

- Heat the oil in a wok over medium heat. Add the spice paste and fry, stirring frequently to avoid burning the sambal. As the sambal dries up, add a little water to loosen up the paste. Cook until the oil separates. This will take at least 45 minutes.

- Add the *asam gelugor* or tamarind juice, salt and dark brown sugar. Let it simmer over low to medium heat, stirring frequently until the oil separates again.

- Taste and adjust the seasoning, if necessary. Add the onion and give it one last stir. Turn the heat off.

- Discard the excess oil, if desired, before serving.

NOTE To make an anchovy sambal, simply fry some dried anchovies until crisp, then drain and set aside. Add the fried anchovies with the onion and mix well.

A Guide to Malaysian Ingredients

There are many ingredients used in Malaysian cooking that contribute to its unique taste and flavour. Most can be found at the local grocery store or Asian supermarkets. For ingredients that may be hard to get a hold of, I have suggested substitutes.

STORE CUPBOARD INGREDIENTS

Candlenuts
Buah Keras

Candlenuts are used widely in Malaysian cooking as a thickening agent. This cream-coloured nut is typically blended into spice pastes to add richness. It is mildly toxic and cannot be consumed raw. If not available, macadamia nuts can be used as a substitute.

Coconut —
Grated or Desiccated, and Toasted
Kerisik

This is an essential ingredient in rendang and other traditional Malaysian dishes. It is made by toasting grated coconut until it is dry and fragrant, then pounding using a mortar and pestle until it becomes a thick, coarse and oily paste. It has a wonderful smoky smell and it creates a distinctive texture and flavour when added to rendangs.

Coconut —
Milk and Cream
Santan

Coconut milk and cream are staples in Malaysian cooking. Coconut cream refers to the cream extracted from grated coconut without added water or using very little water. Coconut milk is thinner and includes a higher water content. I prefer to use coconut milk over coconut cream as the flavours are more subtle. I find that coconut cream tends to overpower my dishes, but you are more than welcome to use coconut cream if you prefer. In Malaysia, I would extract my own coconut milk from freshly grated coconut, but it is also readily available in cans and cartons from supermarkets.

Dried Anchovies
Ikan Bilis

A must-have ingredient in any pantry! These are available at most Asian supermarkets and I use them to flavour stir-fries and jazz up fried rice. They are also great added to sambal. Soaking the dried anchovies in water for 5 minutes helps soften them and makes them less salty.

Dried Chilli Paste
Cili Boh

This is probably one of the most frequently used ingredients in Malaysian households. It is made by boiling and blending dried chillies. You can jazz the paste up by adding garlic, oil or salt, but the basic recipe on page 16 is the one I use in all my recipes.

Dried Shrimps
Udang Kering

Dried shrimps vary from state to state in Malaysia and I personally prefer the ones from the north of Malaysia. They are fragrant without being too overpowering. To use, soak the dried shrimp in water for 5 minutes to rehydrate them before pounding using a mortar and pestle.

Asam Gelugor
Asam Keping

Also known as *asam keping* or dried tamarind skin, *asam gelugor* is used as a souring agent in Asian cooking. This is actually the fruit of the Garcinia atroviridis. The ripened fruit is sliced thinly, then sun-dried and packed for sale. *Asam gelugor* can be purchased at most Asian supermarkets. Substitute with tamarind juice which can be found in local grocery stores.

Fermented Prawn Paste
Belacan

The smell of this paste can be overwhelming on its own, yet when it is added to dishes, it takes the dish to a whole new level in terms of taste and aroma. This pungent paste is made by fermenting tiny shrimp with salt for several weeks. Fermented prawn paste can be a greyish pink or brown, and can come in several forms: cubes, discs, slabs and granules. Except for granules, it is best to toast the paste in a dry pan before using. If the smell is too strong for your liking, omit it.

Palm Sugar
Gula Melaka

Palm sugar is made from the sap of certain palm trees. It comes in cylindrical blocks or discs and goes by different names in different parts of Malaysia. The more common names include *gula Melaka, gula kerek* and *gula manisan*. It is similar in taste to Indian jaggery but darker and not as sweet. Slice, chop or shave off the amount needed.

Peanuts
Kacang Tanah

Peanuts are a key ingredient in satay sauce. Traditionally, making peanut sauce involved a tedious process of roasting, cooling, and then peeling the skins off the peanuts. I've simplified the process by using roasted salted peanuts from my local supermarket. It still results in the same great tasting sauce! As long as you have the right balance of spice and chillies, you can't go wrong.

Rice — Long Grain
Beras

Rice is a staple food in Malaysia and it goes well with all the curries and sambals in this book. My personal preference is basmati rice as it is not only easier to cook, it is also less starchy compared to jasmine rice. Basmati rice has a longer grain than other types of rice and it fluffs up beautifully when cooked.

Rice — Glutinous
Beras Pulut

This is a long grain glutinous rice that is used to make desserts and festive dishes in Malaysia. It is similar to Thai glutinous rice used to make Thai desserts and you should be able to find it in Asian supermarkets. Note that this long grain glutinous rice is different from the short grain sticky rice used in Japanese and Korean cooking.

Soy Sauces — Light (Salty) and Sweet
Kicap Masin dan Kicap Manis

This gem of an ingredient has so many variations — light (salty), sweet, dark and even caramelised varieties. It is the product of a complex process of fermenting soy beans introduced from China in ancient times, and it has become a staple in Malaysian cuisine. You will be able to find this quite easily at Asian supermarkets. I always have bottles of light and sweet soy sauces in my pantry as they are great for seasoning dishes or marinating meats.

FRESH INGREDIENTS

Chillies — Bird's Eye
Cili Padi

Bird's eye chillies are also known as little devil chillies. They are an essential ingredient in making curries, rendangs and sambals to give the dishes a chilli kick. They are tiny, but fiery hot and have an intense flavour. Just a few goes a long way. I indicate green or red bird's eye chillies in recipes where the colour makes a difference, but in many of the recipes, you can choose to use either. I use whatever is available.

Curry Leaves
Daun Kari

Widely available around the globe, curry leaves are commonly used in Indian cuisine. Since Malaysia has a large Indian population, it is no wonder that curry leaves have become a staple ingredient in Malay cooking too. Dried curry leaves can be used in place of fresh ones if the latter is not available. I usually buy the fresh leaves in bulk and freeze them. Strip the leaves from the stem before using.

Galangal
Lengkuas

A member of the ginger family, fresh galangal is readily available from Asian supermarkets, probably arranged alongside ginger. But it can be distinguished from ginger by its lighter skin and whiter flesh. Its flavour is sweet and somewhat peppery, and it is an essential ingredient in rendang dishes. There is no substitute for galangal.

Kaffir Lime Leaves
Daun Limau Purut

Kaffir lime leaves can be easily identified as they are stiff, dark green and shiny, and look like two leaves joined end to end. It can be added whole or finely sliced to add a bright citrus flavour to dishes. There is no substitute for kaffir lime leaves. Like curry leaves, kaffir lime leaves can be frozen.

Laksa Leaves
Daun Kesum

Also known as Vietnamese mint, Vietnamese coriander and *daun kesum* in Malay, these long, slender, pointed leaves have a distinctive citrus aroma. This herb is a must-have ingredient in laksa, hence its common name. A member of the mint family, laksa leaves are often used as a garnish and can also be eaten raw in salads.

Lemongrass
Serai

Classified as a herb, lemongrass has a mild, sweet citrusy flavour that is best released by bruising the bulbous end. It is used widely in Malaysian cooking especially in rendang. To prepare, first peel off the outer layers of leaves, then cut off the top green part, leaving the bottom white part. Depending on the recipe, the lemongrass can then be bruised, chopped or blended as part of a spice paste. I usually buy lemongrass in bulk, prepare them and store them in the freezer. Lemongrass is readily available fresh or frozen from Asian supermarkets.

Pandan Leaves
Daun Pandan

Also known as screw pine leaves, these long, thin and narrow leaves are used widely in South East Asian cooking for its distinctive floral aroma and appetising green colour. To extract both colour and flavour, the leaves can be blended with water and strained to remove the fibre. They can also be added whole, but first knotted, and in the process, bruised, then placed into the pot when cooking rice or syrups for desserts. It is available fresh or frozen in Asian supermarkets.

Torch Ginger Bud
Bunga Kantan

A member of the ginger family, this herb is also known as ginger flower. Easily recognisable by its bright pink flower buds, torch ginger has a distinctive sweet floral aroma with a hint of citrus. To use, peel off the outer layers. The bud can then be sliced thinly for garnish or used whole to flavour gravies.

Turmeric Leaves
Daun Kunyit

These long green leaves of the turmeric plant are used in cooking for their bright floral fragrance and gingery flavour. It is an essential ingredient for certain types of rendang, but if it is not available, kaffir lime leaves can be used in its place. They may not always be available, so when I see them in the supermarkets, I buy and freeze them.

Top: A dried seafood stall at a market in Bangsar, Kuala Lumpur. *Above:* Fresh prawns for sale at the same market.

Weights and Measures

Quantities for this book are given in Metric, Imperial and American (spoon) measures. Standard spoon and cup measurements used are: 1 tsp = 5 ml, 1 Tbsp = 15 ml, 1 cup = 250 ml. All measures are level unless otherwise stated.

LIQUID AND VOLUME MEASURES

Metric	Imperial	American
5 ml	$^1/_6$ fl oz	1 teaspoon
10 ml	$^1/_3$ fl oz	1 dessertspoon
15 ml	$^1/_2$ fl oz	1 tablespoon
60 ml	2 fl oz	$^1/_4$ cup (4 tablespoons)
85 ml	$2^1/_2$ fl oz	$^1/_3$ cup
90 ml	3 fl oz	$^3/_8$ cup (6 tablespoons)
125 ml	4 fl oz	$^1/_2$ cup
180 ml	6 fl oz	$^3/_4$ cup
250 ml	8 fl oz	1 cup
300 ml	10 fl oz ($^1/_2$ pint)	$1^1/_4$ cups
375 ml	12 fl oz	$1^1/_2$ cups
435 ml	14 fl oz	$1^3/_4$ cups
500 ml	16 fl oz	2 cups
625 ml	20 fl oz (1 pint)	$2^1/_2$ cups
750 ml	24 fl oz ($1^1/_5$ pints)	3 cups
1 litre	32 fl oz ($1^3/_5$ pints)	4 cups
1.25 litres	40 fl oz (2 pints)	5 cups
1.5 litres	48 fl oz ($2^2/_5$ pints)	6 cups
2.5 litres	80 fl oz (4 pints)	10 cups

DRY MEASURES

Metric	Imperial
30 grams	1 ounce
45 grams	$1^1/_2$ ounces
55 grams	2 ounces
70 grams	$2^1/_2$ ounces
85 grams	3 ounces
100 grams	$3^1/_2$ ounces
110 grams	4 ounces
125 grams	$4^1/_2$ ounces
140 grams	5 ounces
280 grams	10 ounces
450 grams	16 ounces (1 pound)
500 grams	1 pound, $1^1/_2$ ounces
700 grams	$1^1/_2$ pounds
800 grams	$1^3/_4$ pounds
1 kilogram	2 pounds, 3 ounces
1.5 kilograms	3 pounds, $4^1/_2$ ounces
2 kilograms	4 pounds, 6 ounces

OVEN TEMPERATURE

	°C	°F	Gas Regulo
Very slow	120	250	1
Slow	150	300	2
Moderately slow	160	325	3
Moderate	180	350	4
Moderately hot	190/200	370/400	5/6
Hot	210/220	410/440	6/7
Very hot	230	450	8
Super hot	250/290	475/550	9/10

LENGTH

Metric	Imperial
0.5 cm	$^1/_4$ inch
1 cm	$^1/_2$ inch
1.5 cm	$^3/_4$ inch
2.5 cm	1 inch

Index